🎖 This journal belongs to:

_____

My

قرآن كريم

Journey
Part One (Juz' 'Amma)

Mustafa Raslan

My Juz' 'Amma Journey

Contents

Introduction	2
Symbol Solved	3
Surahs of the Juz'	5
Brief Tajweed Notes	97

An-Naba'	5	An-Nazi'at	10	Abas	18
At-Takweer	21	Al-Infitar	26	Al-Mutafefeen	26
Al-Inshiqaq	34	Al-Burooj	37	At-Tariq	42
Al-A'la	42	Al-Ghashiyah	45	Al-Fajr	50
Al-Balad	53	Ash-Shams	58	Al-Lail	58
Ad-Duha	61	Ash-Sharh	61	At-Teen	66
Al-'Alaq	66	Al-Qadr	69	Al-Baiynah	69
Az-Zalzalah	74	Al-'Adiyat	74	Al-Qari'ah	77
At-Takathur	77	Al-'Asr	82	Al-Humazah	82
Al-Feel	82	Quraysh	85	Al-Ma'oon	85
Al-Kawthar	85	Al-Kafiroon	90	An-Nasr	90
Al-Masad	90	Al-Ikhlas	93	Al-Falaq	93
		An-Nas	93		

My Juz' 'Amma Journey

Introduction

Allah سُبْحَانَهُ وَتَعَالَى has revealed the Qur'an as guidance for us. And in order to get this guidance fully, we have to learn the Qur'an. Learning the Qur'an is a beautiful journey. And it is meant to be entertaining and full of benefits.

The first part you should start learning is Juz' 'Amma (part 30) which includes the shortest surahs in the Qur'an. And in order to learn it in a comprehensive way, this book is made to help you learn, understand, reflect on, write, and memorize the surahs of Juz' 'Amma.

How to use the book[1]

Before you start learning any surah, learn some facts about it. Check the book contents. When you go to the Quran pages, you will notice that each page in the juz' occupies four pages in this book:
❶ The Quranic page that you will work on.
❷ The meanings of the ayahs, linked to icons to remember.
❸ Tajweed analysis assignment, and memorization tracker
❹ Track with your pen the Arabic writing.

You don't have to work on a full page at a time. You can divide it into lines or ayahs according to your ability.

Don't move to the next page until you master the current one.

After you understand the ayahs, take some minutes to reflect on them and write down what you get. Look for the reflection icon.

Set a target to yourself. For example, three lines every day.

Join the pages together, i.e. when you complete page two, revise it with page one, etc.

Better to find a group of people to join you in this inspiring journey.

---

[1] The pages order in this book matches the pages order in the Qur'an. For example, the first page of Surah al-Naba does exist on the left side of Mushaf al-Madinah. You will find it here on the left side as well.
All icons in this book are taken from the free icons' website www.flaticon.com.

My Juz' 'Amma Journey

Symbols Solved

Listen and read
First thing first, you should read the ayahs you intend to learn as correct as possible. Repeat behind a teacher or a reciter.

Tajweed analysis
Analysing Tajweed rules is the best way to be perfect in Tajweed. Get out as much as you can of the words under their matching space.

Tafseer
Read or listen to the explanation. Put your understanding and reflections.

Writing
Track with your pen on the washed-out grayscale image of the Qur'an.

Memorizing
Repeat each line 25 times.[2] Mark one smiley face every time you repeat. Then move to the next line, and so on.

Reflect
This is your space. Write down your reflections or some beneficial points regarding some of the verses in the page. You will find its box next to the Qur'an pages.

Hifdh Notes
While you are memorizing, sometimes you will need to make some notes about some mistakes in your hifdh. Use the space with this icon.

---

[2] It is proven that the thing you repeat 40 times gets strong in your head, no matter how weak your memory is. Work on every ayah many times and tick a box every time you repeat it.

Let's start our journey!

الجزء الثلاثون — سورة النبأ

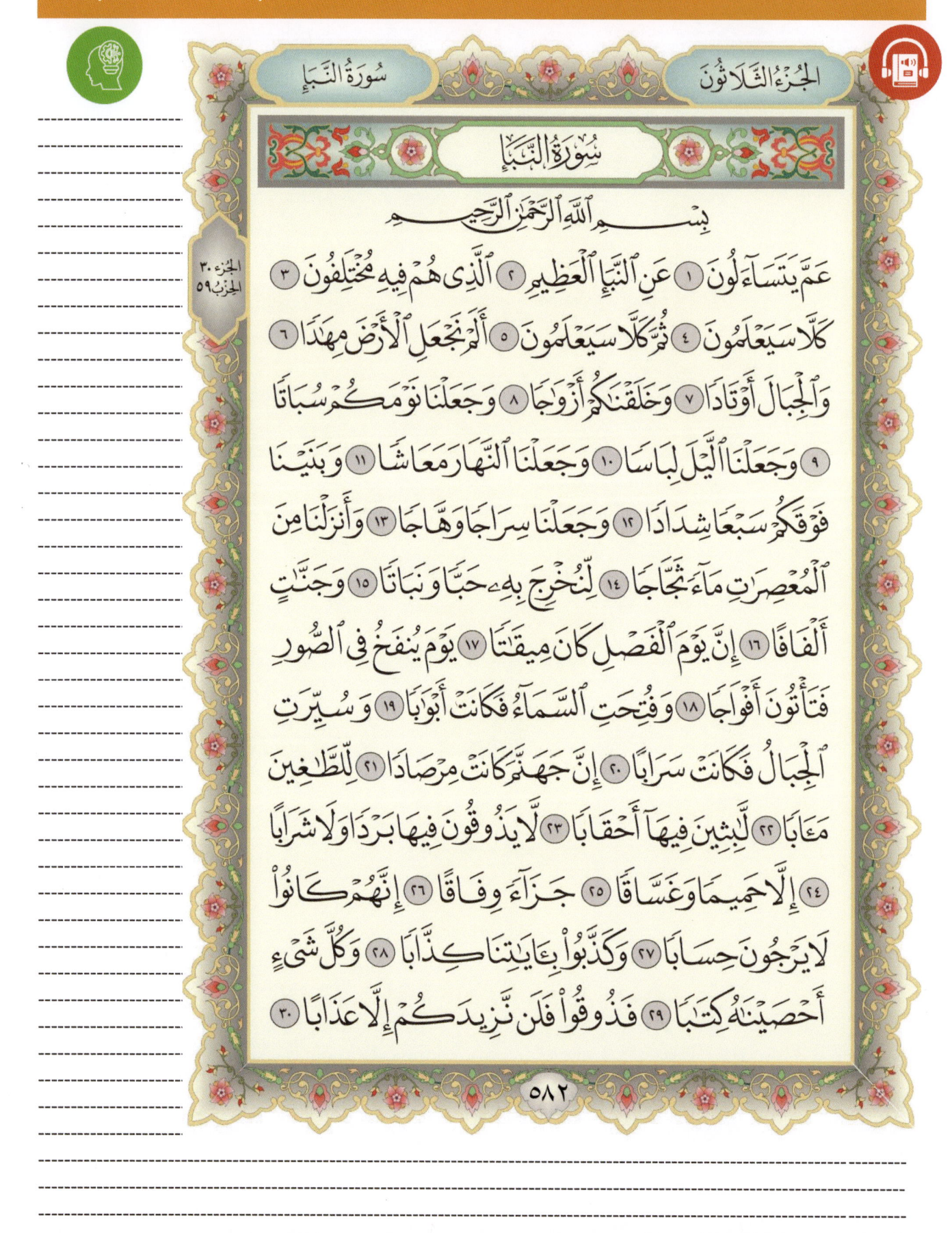

سُورَةُ النَّبَإِ

بِسْمِ اللَّهِ الرَّحْمَٰنِ الرَّحِيمِ

عَمَّ يَتَسَاءَلُونَ ﴿١﴾ عَنِ النَّبَإِ الْعَظِيمِ ﴿٢﴾ الَّذِي هُمْ فِيهِ مُخْتَلِفُونَ ﴿٣﴾ كَلَّا سَيَعْلَمُونَ ﴿٤﴾ ثُمَّ كَلَّا سَيَعْلَمُونَ ﴿٥﴾ أَلَمْ نَجْعَلِ الْأَرْضَ مِهَادًا ﴿٦﴾ وَالْجِبَالَ أَوْتَادًا ﴿٧﴾ وَخَلَقْنَاكُمْ أَزْوَاجًا ﴿٨﴾ وَجَعَلْنَا نَوْمَكُمْ سُبَاتًا ﴿٩﴾ وَجَعَلْنَا اللَّيْلَ لِبَاسًا ﴿١٠﴾ وَجَعَلْنَا النَّهَارَ مَعَاشًا ﴿١١﴾ وَبَنَيْنَا فَوْقَكُمْ سَبْعًا شِدَادًا ﴿١٢﴾ وَجَعَلْنَا سِرَاجًا وَهَّاجًا ﴿١٣﴾ وَأَنزَلْنَا مِنَ الْمُعْصِرَاتِ مَاءً ثَجَّاجًا ﴿١٤﴾ لِنُخْرِجَ بِهِ حَبًّا وَنَبَاتًا ﴿١٥﴾ وَجَنَّاتٍ أَلْفَافًا ﴿١٦﴾ إِنَّ يَوْمَ الْفَصْلِ كَانَ مِيقَاتًا ﴿١٧﴾ يَوْمَ يُنفَخُ فِي الصُّورِ فَتَأْتُونَ أَفْوَاجًا ﴿١٨﴾ وَفُتِحَتِ السَّمَاءُ فَكَانَتْ أَبْوَابًا ﴿١٩﴾ وَسُيِّرَتِ الْجِبَالُ فَكَانَتْ سَرَابًا ﴿٢٠﴾ إِنَّ جَهَنَّمَ كَانَتْ مِرْصَادًا ﴿٢١﴾ لِلطَّاغِينَ مَآبًا ﴿٢٢﴾ لَابِثِينَ فِيهَا أَحْقَابًا ﴿٢٣﴾ لَا يَذُوقُونَ فِيهَا بَرْدًا وَلَا شَرَابًا ﴿٢٤﴾ إِلَّا حَمِيمًا وَغَسَّاقًا ﴿٢٥﴾ جَزَاءً وِفَاقًا ﴿٢٦﴾ إِنَّهُمْ كَانُوا لَا يَرْجُونَ حِسَابًا ﴿٢٧﴾ وَكَذَّبُوا بِآيَاتِنَا كِذَّابًا ﴿٢٨﴾ وَكُلَّ شَيْءٍ أَحْصَيْنَاهُ كِتَابًا ﴿٢٩﴾ فَذُوقُوا فَلَن نَّزِيدَكُمْ إِلَّا عَذَابًا ﴿٣٠﴾

٥٨٢

My Juz' 'Amma Journey

Surah an-Naba' answers the disbelievers who disputed about the fact of resurrection. It also tells us about the different people on that Day.

	1-5. About what are the disbelievers asking one another? About the great news around which they dispute. Indeed, they are going to know.		
	6. Have We not made the earth a resting place?		7. And have We not made the mountains as stakes?
	8. And We created you in pairs.		9. And We made your sleep a means for rest.
	10. And We made the night as clothing that covers you.		11. And We made the day for livelihood.
	12. And We constructed above you seven strong heavens.		13. And We made therein a burning lamp.
	14-16. And We sent down, from the clouds, pouring water; so that We may bring forth thereby grain, vegetation and gardens of entwined growth.		
	17. Indeed, the Day of Judgement is an appointed time.		18. It is the Day when the Horn is blown, and you will come forth in multitudes.
	19. And the heaven is opened and becomes gateways.		20. And the mountains are removed and will be just a mirage.
	21-23. Indeed, the Hell has been lying in wait as a place of return for the transgressors, in which they will remain for ages unending.		
	24-26. They will not taste therein any coolness or drink, except boiling water and the pus; an appropriate recompense.		
	27, 28. Indeed, they were not expecting any account, and denied Our verses completely.		29. But We have listed all things in writing.
	30. So, taste the penalty, and We will only increase you in torment.		

الجزءُ الثلاثونَ سُورَةُ النَّبَأِ

سُورَةُ النَّبَأِ

بِسْمِ اللَّهِ الرَّحْمَٰنِ الرَّحِيمِ

عَمَّ يَتَسَاءَلُونَ ۝ عَنِ النَّبَإِ الْعَظِيمِ ۝ الَّذِي هُمْ فِيهِ مُخْتَلِفُونَ ۝ كَلَّا سَيَعْلَمُونَ ۝ ثُمَّ كَلَّا سَيَعْلَمُونَ ۝ أَلَمْ نَجْعَلِ الْأَرْضَ مِهَادًا ۝ وَالْجِبَالَ أَوْتَادًا ۝ وَخَلَقْنَاكُمْ أَزْوَاجًا ۝ وَجَعَلْنَا نَوْمَكُمْ سُبَاتًا ۝ وَجَعَلْنَا اللَّيْلَ لِبَاسًا ۝ وَجَعَلْنَا النَّهَارَ مَعَاشًا ۝ وَبَنَيْنَا فَوْقَكُمْ سَبْعًا شِدَادًا ۝ وَجَعَلْنَا سِرَاجًا وَهَّاجًا ۝ وَأَنْزَلْنَا مِنَ الْمُعْصِرَاتِ مَاءً ثَجَّاجًا ۝ لِنُخْرِجَ بِهِ حَبًّا وَنَبَاتًا ۝ وَجَنَّاتٍ أَلْفَافًا ۝ إِنَّ يَوْمَ الْفَصْلِ كَانَ مِيقَاتًا ۝ يَوْمَ يُنْفَخُ فِي الصُّورِ فَتَأْتُونَ أَفْوَاجًا ۝ وَفُتِحَتِ السَّمَاءُ فَكَانَتْ أَبْوَابًا ۝ وَسُيِّرَتِ الْجِبَالُ فَكَانَتْ سَرَابًا ۝ إِنَّ جَهَنَّمَ كَانَتْ مِرْصَادًا ۝ لِلطَّاغِينَ مَآبًا ۝ لَابِثِينَ فِيهَا أَحْقَابًا ۝ لَا يَذُوقُونَ فِيهَا بَرْدًا وَلَا شَرَابًا ۝ إِلَّا حَمِيمًا وَغَسَّاقًا ۝ جَزَاءً وِفَاقًا ۝ إِنَّهُمْ كَانُوا لَا يَرْجُونَ حِسَابًا ۝ وَكَذَّبُوا بِآيَاتِنَا كِذَّابًا ۝ وَكُلَّ شَيْءٍ أَحْصَيْنَاهُ كِتَابًا ۝ فَذُوقُوا فَلَنْ نَزِيدَكُمْ إِلَّا عَذَابًا ۝

٥٨٢

My Juz' 'Amma Journey

Write down as many examples as you can from the page:

Identify Makharij of 6 letters	Ghunnah	Madd	Elevated sounds
----------	----------	----------	----------

Noon Saakin & Tanween	Meem Saakin	Qalqalah	Hamzatul-wasl
Idgham: ----------	Idgham: ----------	----------	----------
Ikhfaa': ----------	Ikhfaa': ----------		
Iqlab: ----------			

8

My Juz' 'Amma Journey

31-34 Indeed, for the righteous is success; gardens, grapevines, beautiful young women of equal age and a cup full of drinks.

35. They will not hear any ill speech or falsehood there.

36. This will be a reward and a generous gift from your Lord, calculated according to the very best of their good deeds.

37, 38. This is from the Lord of the heavens and the earth and whatever is between them, the Most Merciful. No one possesses authority for speech without His permission, on the Day when Jibril and the angels will stand in rows. None of them will speak except after the Most Merciful permits, and they will have to speak only the truth.

39, 40. That will be the True Day. So, whoever wants to go to his Lord in a pleasing way, let him do this now. Indeed, We have warned you of a near punishment, on the Day when a man will observe what he has put forth, and the disbeliever will say, "Oh, I wish that I were dust!"

Surah an-Nazi'at reminds us of Allah and the Day of Judgment.

1. By the angels, who extract the disbelievers' souls fiercely,

2. And by the angels who take the believers' souls nicely,

3. And by the angels who glide between heavens and earth as if swimming,

4. And by the angels who race each other in Allah's obedience.

5. And by the angels who arrange the matters they are entitled for,

6, 7. When a Day will come for the blast of the Horn to convulse the creation, followed by the second blast,

8. Hearts, then, will tremble,

9. And eyes will be humbled.

10-12. The disbelievers say in mockery: "Will we indeed be returned to our former state of life Even after we become decayed bones? That, then, would be a losing return!"

13. Indeed, it will be just one shout,

14. And then they will be back to life on the earth's surface.

15, 16. Did you know the story of Musa, when his Lord called to him in the sacred valley of Tuwa in Sinai?

الجزء الثلاثون — سورة النبأ

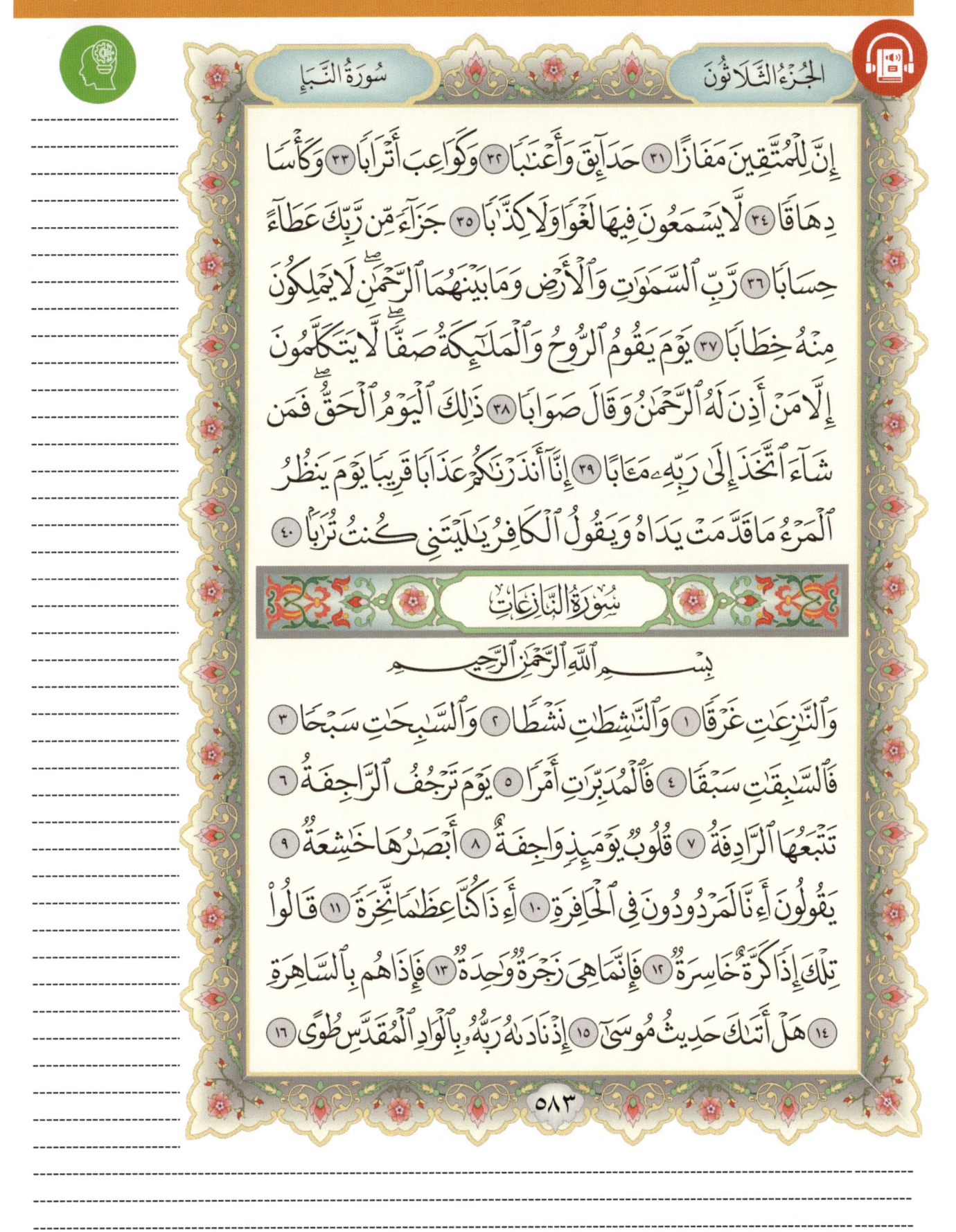

إِنَّ لِلْمُتَّقِينَ مَفَازًا ۝ حَدَائِقَ وَأَعْنَابًا ۝ وَكَوَاعِبَ أَتْرَابًا ۝ وَكَأْسًا دِهَاقًا ۝ لَّا يَسْمَعُونَ فِيهَا لَغْوًا وَلَا كِذَّابًا ۝ جَزَاءً مِّن رَّبِّكَ عَطَاءً حِسَابًا ۝ رَّبِّ السَّمَاوَاتِ وَالْأَرْضِ وَمَا بَيْنَهُمَا الرَّحْمَٰنِ ۖ لَا يَمْلِكُونَ مِنْهُ خِطَابًا ۝ يَوْمَ يَقُومُ الرُّوحُ وَالْمَلَائِكَةُ صَفًّا ۖ لَّا يَتَكَلَّمُونَ إِلَّا مَنْ أَذِنَ لَهُ الرَّحْمَٰنُ وَقَالَ صَوَابًا ۝ ذَٰلِكَ الْيَوْمُ الْحَقُّ ۖ فَمَن شَاءَ اتَّخَذَ إِلَىٰ رَبِّهِ مَآبًا ۝ إِنَّا أَنذَرْنَاكُمْ عَذَابًا قَرِيبًا يَوْمَ يَنظُرُ الْمَرْءُ مَا قَدَّمَتْ يَدَاهُ وَيَقُولُ الْكَافِرُ يَا لَيْتَنِي كُنتُ تُرَابًا ۝

سورة النازعات

بِسْمِ اللَّهِ الرَّحْمَٰنِ الرَّحِيمِ

وَالنَّازِعَاتِ غَرْقًا ۝ وَالنَّاشِطَاتِ نَشْطًا ۝ وَالسَّابِحَاتِ سَبْحًا ۝ فَالسَّابِقَاتِ سَبْقًا ۝ فَالْمُدَبِّرَاتِ أَمْرًا ۝ يَوْمَ تَرْجُفُ الرَّاجِفَةُ ۝ تَتْبَعُهَا الرَّادِفَةُ ۝ قُلُوبٌ يَوْمَئِذٍ وَاجِفَةٌ ۝ أَبْصَارُهَا خَاشِعَةٌ ۝ يَقُولُونَ أَإِنَّا لَمَرْدُودُونَ فِي الْحَافِرَةِ ۝ أَإِذَا كُنَّا عِظَامًا نَّخِرَةً ۝ قَالُوا تِلْكَ إِذًا كَرَّةٌ خَاسِرَةٌ ۝ فَإِنَّمَا هِيَ زَجْرَةٌ وَاحِدَةٌ ۝ فَإِذَا هُم بِالسَّاهِرَةِ ۝ هَلْ أَتَاكَ حَدِيثُ مُوسَىٰ ۝ إِذْ نَادَاهُ رَبُّهُ بِالْوَادِ الْمُقَدَّسِ طُوًى ۝

٥٨٣

My Juz' 'Amma Journey

Write down as many examples as you can from the page:

Identify Makharij of 6 letters	Ghunnah	Madd	Elevated sounds
------------------- ------------------- ------------------- ------------------- ------------------- -------------------	------------------- ------------------- ------------------- ------------------- ------------------- -------------------	------------------- ------------------- ------------------- ------------------- ------------------- -------------------	------------------- ------------------- ------------------- ------------------- ------------------- -------------------

Noon Saakin & Tanween	Meem Saakin	Qalqalah	Hamzatul-wasl
Idgham: ----------------- ----------------- Ikhfaa': ----------------- ----------------- Iqlab: -----------------	Idgham: ----------------- ----------------- Ikhfaa': ----------------- -----------------	----------------- ----------------- ----------------- -----------------	----------------- ----------------- ----------------- -----------------

11

الجزء الثلاثون — سورة النبأ

إِنَّ لِلْمُتَّقِينَ مَفَازًا ۝ حَدَائِقَ وَأَعْنَابًا ۝ وَكَوَاعِبَ أَتْرَابًا ۝ وَكَأْسًا دِهَاقًا ۝ لَا يَسْمَعُونَ فِيهَا لَغْوًا وَلَا كِذَّابًا ۝ جَزَاءً مِّن رَّبِّكَ عَطَاءً حِسَابًا ۝ رَّبِّ السَّمَاوَاتِ وَالْأَرْضِ وَمَا بَيْنَهُمَا الرَّحْمَٰنِ لَا يَمْلِكُونَ مِنْهُ خِطَابًا ۝ يَوْمَ يَقُومُ الرُّوحُ وَالْمَلَائِكَةُ صَفًّا لَّا يَتَكَلَّمُونَ إِلَّا مَنْ أَذِنَ لَهُ الرَّحْمَٰنُ وَقَالَ صَوَابًا ۝ ذَٰلِكَ الْيَوْمُ الْحَقُّ فَمَن شَاءَ اتَّخَذَ إِلَىٰ رَبِّهِ مَآبًا ۝ إِنَّا أَنذَرْنَاكُمْ عَذَابًا قَرِيبًا يَوْمَ يَنظُرُ الْمَرْءُ مَا قَدَّمَتْ يَدَاهُ وَيَقُولُ الْكَافِرُ يَا لَيْتَنِي كُنتُ تُرَابًا ۝

سورة النازعات

بِسْمِ اللَّهِ الرَّحْمَٰنِ الرَّحِيمِ

وَالنَّازِعَاتِ غَرْقًا ۝ وَالنَّاشِطَاتِ نَشْطًا ۝ وَالسَّابِحَاتِ سَبْحًا ۝ فَالسَّابِقَاتِ سَبْقًا ۝ فَالْمُدَبِّرَاتِ أَمْرًا ۝ يَوْمَ تَرْجُفُ الرَّاجِفَةُ ۝ تَتْبَعُهَا الرَّادِفَةُ ۝ قُلُوبٌ يَوْمَئِذٍ وَاجِفَةٌ ۝ أَبْصَارُهَا خَاشِعَةٌ ۝ يَقُولُونَ أَإِنَّا لَمَرْدُودُونَ فِي الْحَافِرَةِ ۝ أَإِذَا كُنَّا عِظَامًا نَّخِرَةً ۝ قَالُوا تِلْكَ إِذًا كَرَّةٌ خَاسِرَةٌ ۝ فَإِنَّمَا هِيَ زَجْرَةٌ وَاحِدَةٌ ۝ فَإِذَا هُم بِالسَّاهِرَةِ ۝ هَلْ أَتَاكَ حَدِيثُ مُوسَىٰ ۝ إِذْ نَادَاهُ رَبُّهُ بِالْوَادِ الْمُقَدَّسِ طُوًى ۝

٥٨٣

My Juz' 'Amma Journey

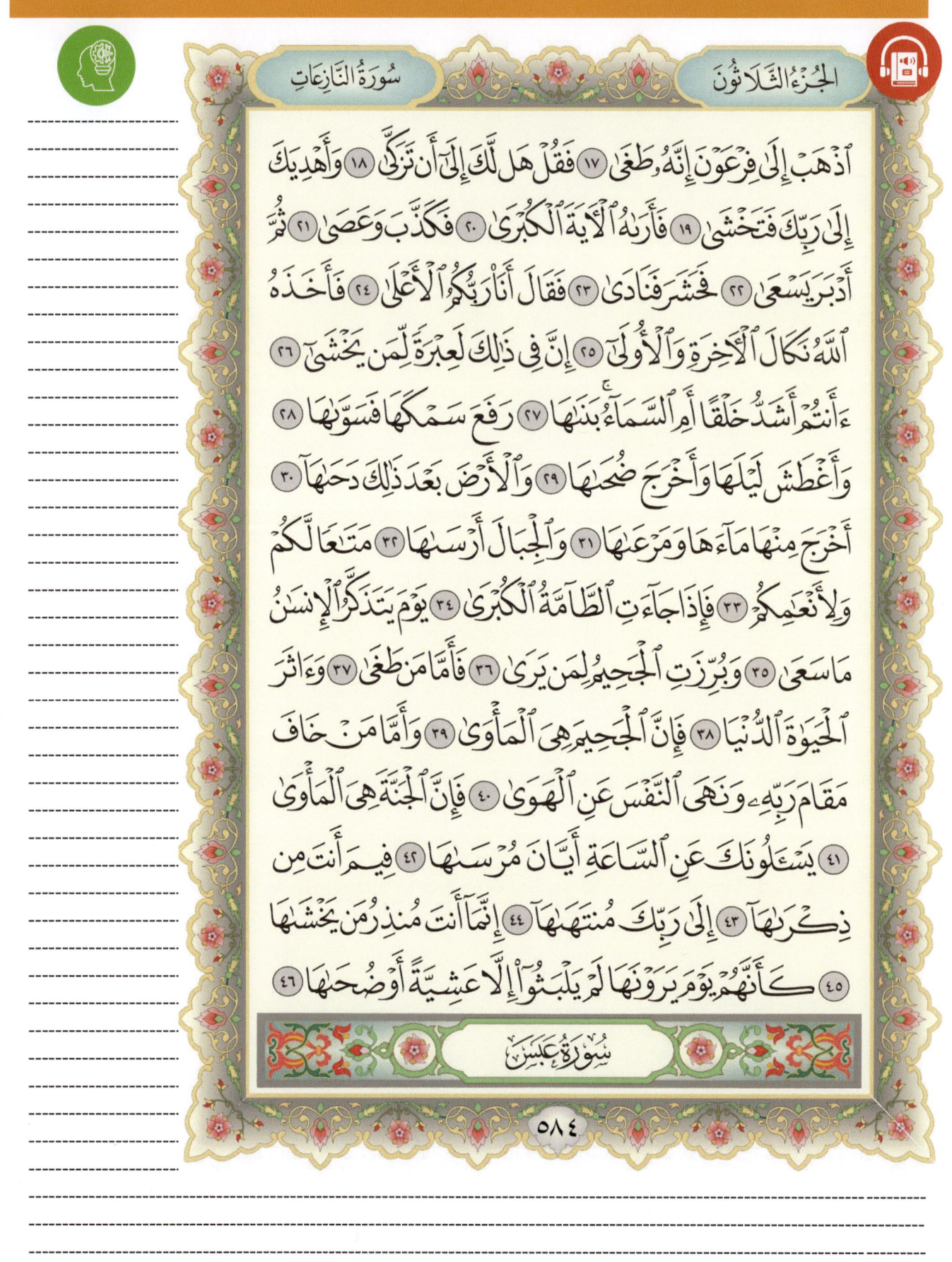

سُورَةُ النَّازِعَاتِ — الجُزْءُ الثَّلَاثُونَ

اذْهَبْ إِلَىٰ فِرْعَوْنَ إِنَّهُ طَغَىٰ ۝١٧ فَقُلْ هَل لَّكَ إِلَىٰ أَن تَزَكَّىٰ ۝١٨ وَأَهْدِيَكَ إِلَىٰ رَبِّكَ فَتَخْشَىٰ ۝١٩ فَأَرَاهُ الْآيَةَ الْكُبْرَىٰ ۝٢٠ فَكَذَّبَ وَعَصَىٰ ۝٢١ ثُمَّ أَدْبَرَ يَسْعَىٰ ۝٢٢ فَحَشَرَ فَنَادَىٰ ۝٢٣ فَقَالَ أَنَا رَبُّكُمُ الْأَعْلَىٰ ۝٢٤ فَأَخَذَهُ اللَّهُ نَكَالَ الْآخِرَةِ وَالْأُولَىٰ ۝٢٥ إِنَّ فِي ذَٰلِكَ لَعِبْرَةً لِّمَن يَخْشَىٰ ۝٢٦ أَأَنتُمْ أَشَدُّ خَلْقًا أَمِ السَّمَاءُ ۚ بَنَاهَا ۝٢٧ رَفَعَ سَمْكَهَا فَسَوَّاهَا ۝٢٨ وَأَغْطَشَ لَيْلَهَا وَأَخْرَجَ ضُحَاهَا ۝٢٩ وَالْأَرْضَ بَعْدَ ذَٰلِكَ دَحَاهَا ۝٣٠ أَخْرَجَ مِنْهَا مَاءَهَا وَمَرْعَاهَا ۝٣١ وَالْجِبَالَ أَرْسَاهَا ۝٣٢ مَتَاعًا لَّكُمْ وَلِأَنْعَامِكُمْ ۝٣٣ فَإِذَا جَاءَتِ الطَّامَّةُ الْكُبْرَىٰ ۝٣٤ يَوْمَ يَتَذَكَّرُ الْإِنسَانُ مَا سَعَىٰ ۝٣٥ وَبُرِّزَتِ الْجَحِيمُ لِمَن يَرَىٰ ۝٣٦ فَأَمَّا مَن طَغَىٰ ۝٣٧ وَآثَرَ الْحَيَاةَ الدُّنْيَا ۝٣٨ فَإِنَّ الْجَحِيمَ هِيَ الْمَأْوَىٰ ۝٣٩ وَأَمَّا مَنْ خَافَ مَقَامَ رَبِّهِ وَنَهَى النَّفْسَ عَنِ الْهَوَىٰ ۝٤٠ فَإِنَّ الْجَنَّةَ هِيَ الْمَأْوَىٰ ۝٤١ يَسْأَلُونَكَ عَنِ السَّاعَةِ أَيَّانَ مُرْسَاهَا ۝٤٢ فِيمَ أَنتَ مِن ذِكْرَاهَا ۝٤٣ إِلَىٰ رَبِّكَ مُنتَهَاهَا ۝٤٤ إِنَّمَا أَنتَ مُنذِرُ مَن يَخْشَاهَا ۝٤٥ كَأَنَّهُمْ يَوْمَ يَرَوْنَهَا لَمْ يَلْبَثُوا إِلَّا عَشِيَّةً أَوْ ضُحَاهَا ۝٤٦

سُورَةُ عَبَسَ

٥٨٤

13

My Juz' 'Amma Journey

17. Allah said to Musa: "Go to Pharaoh. Indeed, he has transgressed.

18, 19. And say to him, 'Would you like to get self-purification and get guided to your Lord so you would fear Him?'"

20. And Musa showed him the greatest sign.

21. But Pharaoh denied and disobeyed.

22-24. Then he turned his back, plotting. And he gathered his people and called out, "I am your most exalted lord."

25. So, Allah seized him and punished him in the world by drowning him in the sea. And He will punish him in the Afterlife by entering him into the severest punishment.

26. Indeed in that is a lesson for whoever would fear Allah.

27. Who is harder in creation, you or the heavens? Allah has constructed it?

28-29. He raised its ceiling and proportioned it. And He darkened its night and extracted its brightness.

30-32. And, after that, He spread the earth. He extracted from it its water and its pasture. And He set the mountains firmly.

33. All that is for your benefit, and for the benefit of your livestock.

34. But when there comes the greatest Overwhelming Calamity,

35. Man, that Day, will remember that for which he strove,

36. And Hellfire will be exposed for all those who see.

37-39. So, as for he who transgressed and preferred the life of the world, then Hellfire will be his refuge.

40-41. And as for the one who feared his standing before his Lord and stopped himself from following his desires, then Paradise will be his refuge.

42. The disbelievers ask you, O Messenger, about the Hour, saying: "When is its arrival?"

43, 44. You have no knowledge you can mention to them regarding this. Only Allah knows it.

45. You are only a warner to the one who fears the Hour, as he is the only one who benefits from this.

46. When the disbelievers see the Hour, it will be for them as if they only remained in the world for a single evening or morning.

My Juz' 'Amma Journey

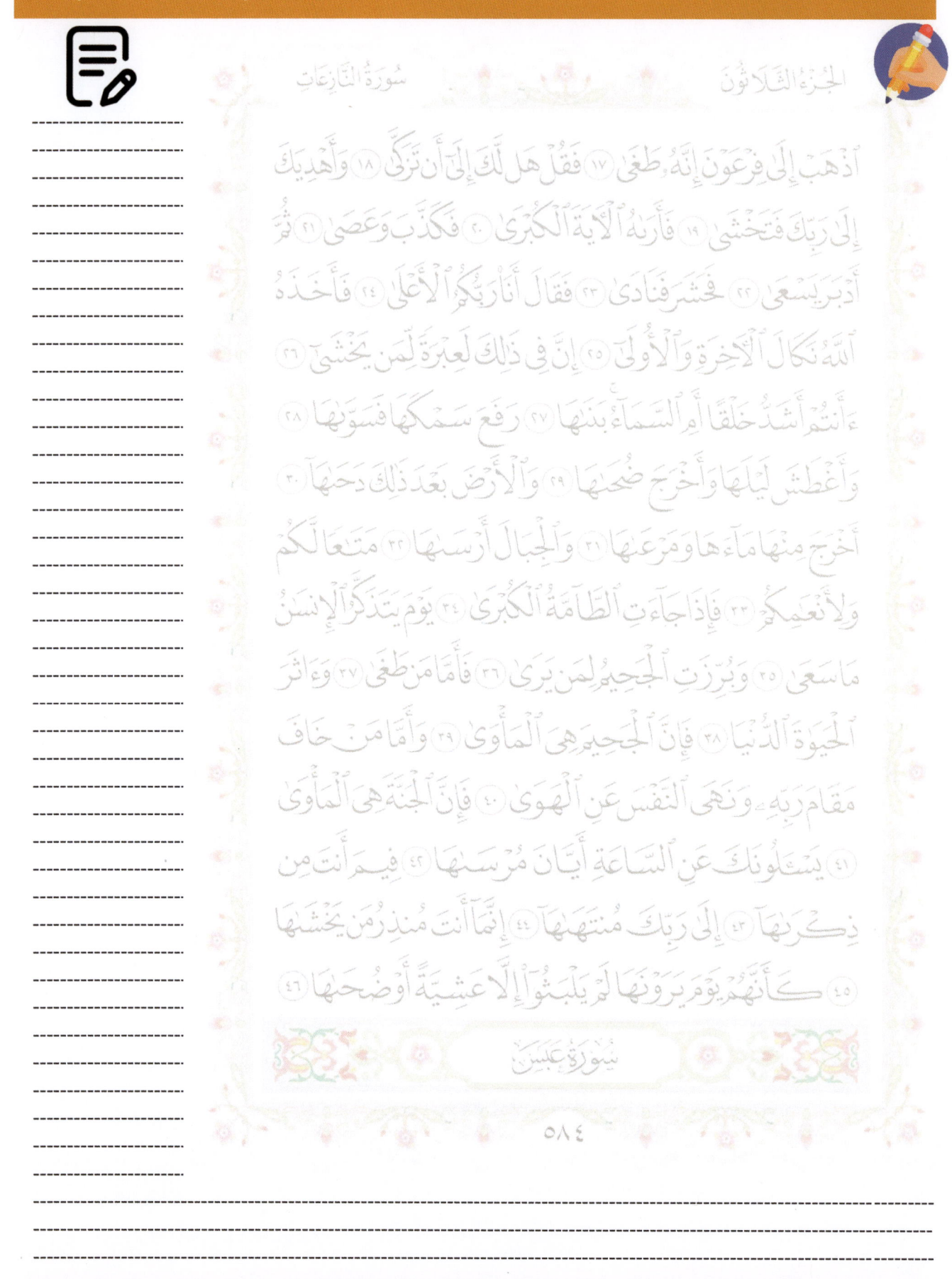

الجزء الثلاثون — سورة النازعات

اذْهَبْ إِلَىٰ فِرْعَوْنَ إِنَّهُ طَغَىٰ ۝ فَقُلْ هَل لَّكَ إِلَىٰ أَن تَزَكَّىٰ ۝ وَأَهْدِيَكَ إِلَىٰ رَبِّكَ فَتَخْشَىٰ ۝ فَأَرَاهُ الْآيَةَ الْكُبْرَىٰ ۝ فَكَذَّبَ وَعَصَىٰ ۝ ثُمَّ أَدْبَرَ يَسْعَىٰ ۝ فَحَشَرَ فَنَادَىٰ ۝ فَقَالَ أَنَا رَبُّكُمُ الْأَعْلَىٰ ۝ فَأَخَذَهُ اللَّهُ نَكَالَ الْآخِرَةِ وَالْأُولَىٰ ۝ إِنَّ فِي ذَٰلِكَ لَعِبْرَةً لِّمَن يَخْشَىٰ ۝ ءَأَنتُمْ أَشَدُّ خَلْقًا أَمِ السَّمَاءُ بَنَاهَا ۝ رَفَعَ سَمْكَهَا فَسَوَّاهَا ۝ وَأَغْطَشَ لَيْلَهَا وَأَخْرَجَ ضُحَاهَا ۝ وَالْأَرْضَ بَعْدَ ذَٰلِكَ دَحَاهَا ۝ أَخْرَجَ مِنْهَا مَاءَهَا وَمَرْعَاهَا ۝ وَالْجِبَالَ أَرْسَاهَا ۝ مَتَاعًا لَّكُمْ وَلِأَنْعَامِكُمْ ۝ فَإِذَا جَاءَتِ الطَّامَّةُ الْكُبْرَىٰ ۝ يَوْمَ يَتَذَكَّرُ الْإِنسَانُ مَا سَعَىٰ ۝ وَبُرِّزَتِ الْجَحِيمُ لِمَن يَرَىٰ ۝ فَأَمَّا مَن طَغَىٰ ۝ وَآثَرَ الْحَيَاةَ الدُّنْيَا ۝ فَإِنَّ الْجَحِيمَ هِيَ الْمَأْوَىٰ ۝ وَأَمَّا مَنْ خَافَ مَقَامَ رَبِّهِ وَنَهَى النَّفْسَ عَنِ الْهَوَىٰ ۝ فَإِنَّ الْجَنَّةَ هِيَ الْمَأْوَىٰ ۝ يَسْأَلُونَكَ عَنِ السَّاعَةِ أَيَّانَ مُرْسَاهَا ۝ فِيمَ أَنتَ مِن ذِكْرَاهَا ۝ إِلَىٰ رَبِّكَ مُنتَهَاهَا ۝ إِنَّمَا أَنتَ مُنذِرُ مَن يَخْشَاهَا ۝ كَأَنَّهُمْ يَوْمَ يَرَوْنَهَا لَمْ يَلْبَثُوا إِلَّا عَشِيَّةً أَوْ ضُحَاهَا ۝

سورة عبس

٥٨٤

My Juz' 'Amma Journey

Write down as many examples as you can from the page:

Identify Makharij of 6 letters	Ghunnah	Madd	Elevated sounds
------------------	------------------	------------------	------------------
------------------	------------------	------------------	------------------
------------------	------------------	------------------	------------------
------------------	------------------	------------------	------------------
------------------	------------------	------------------	------------------
------------------	------------------	------------------	------------------

Noon Saakin & Tanween	Meem Saakin	Qalqalah	Hamzatul-wasl
Idgham: -------------	Idgham: -----------	------------------	------------------
Ikhfaa': ------------	Ikhfaa': ----------	------------------	------------------
Iqlab: --------------		------------------	------------------

My Juz' 'Amma Journey

Surah Abas reminds the disbelievers with the many proofs and assuring them that they cannot live peacefully without believing in their Creator!

1-2. The Prophet ﷺ frowned and turned away when Abdullah ibn Umm-Maktum, a blind companion, came to him while he ﷺ was preaching to some of the Quraish chiefs.
3-4. What could tell you that per chance the blind might increase in self-purification or receive admonition that would benefit him?
5-6. As for him who thinks himself self-sufficient, you gave him attention;

	7. What does it matter to you if he won't get self-purification.		8-10. But as to him who came to you running, fearing Allah's Punishment, you ignored him!
	11-12. Nay, indeed these verses of this Qur'an are an admonition, so whoever wills, let him pay attention to it.		13–16. This admonition is in Scrolls, held in honour with Allah, raised high, purified, and carried by noble and dutiful angels.
	17. Be cursed the disbelieving man! How ungrateful he is!		18-19. Does not he reflect on what Allah creates him from? From semen drops, and then sets him in due proportion.
	20. Then He makes the path of distinguishing between good and evil easy for him.		21. Then He causes him to die and puts him in the grave.
	22. Then, when it is Allah's Will, He will resurrect him again.		23. And yet, man has not done what Allah commanded him.

	24-32. Then let man look at his food; that We send rain in abundance, then We split the earth in clefts, then We cause therein the grain, grapes, clover, olives, date-palms, dense gardens, fruits and herbage to grow; to be a provision for you and your cattle.

	33-36. Then, when there comes the Day of the second blowing of the Trumpet, man shall flee from his brother, mother, father, wife and children.		37-40. Everyman, that Day, will have enough to make him careless of others. Some faces that Day, will be bright and rejoicing. And other faces will be dust-stained.

الجزء الثلاثون — سورة عبس

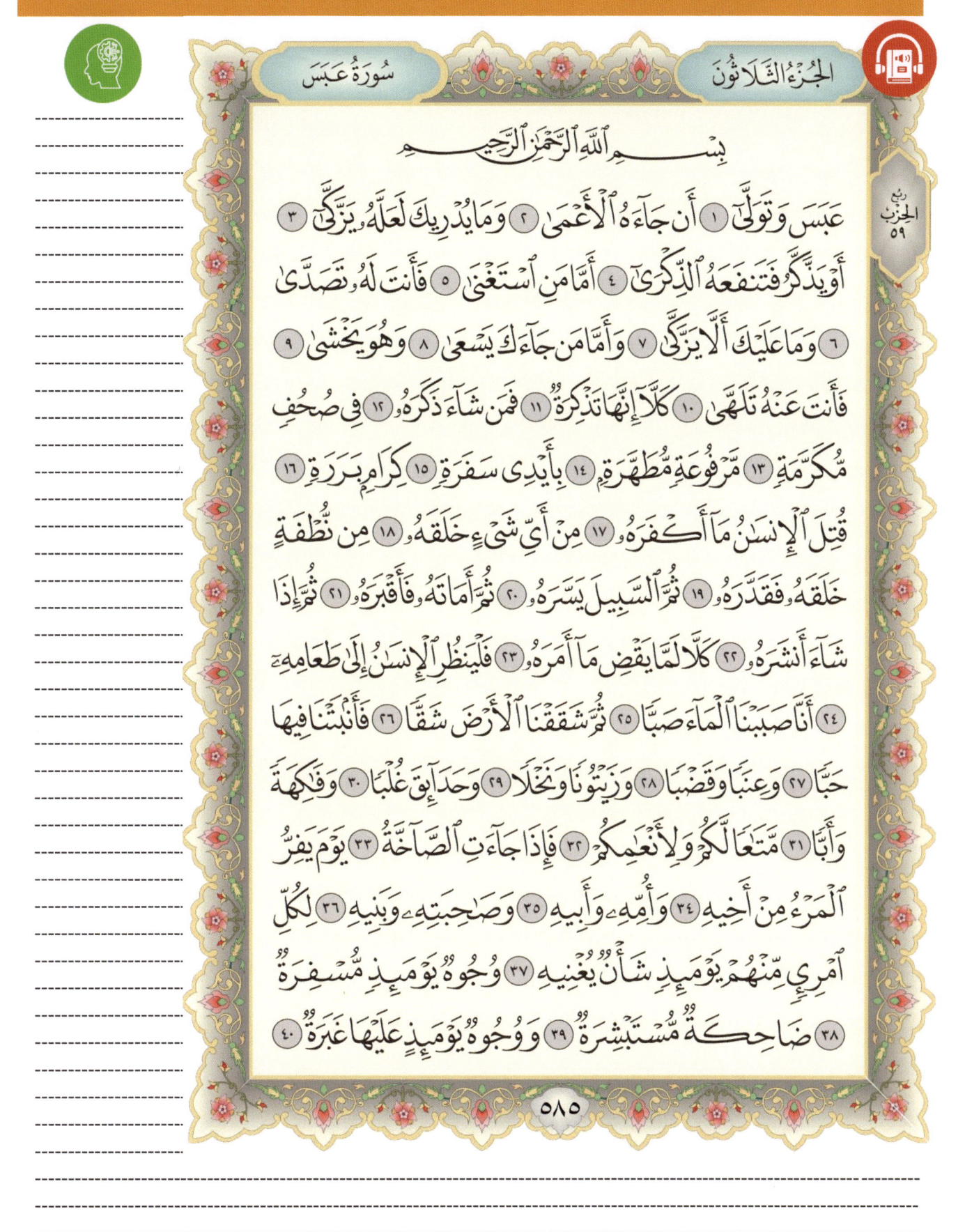

بِسْمِ اللَّهِ الرَّحْمَٰنِ الرَّحِيمِ

عَبَسَ وَتَوَلَّىٰ ۝١ أَن جَاءَهُ الْأَعْمَىٰ ۝٢ وَمَا يُدْرِيكَ لَعَلَّهُ يَزَّكَّىٰ ۝٣ أَوْ يَذَّكَّرُ فَتَنفَعَهُ الذِّكْرَىٰ ۝٤ أَمَّا مَنِ اسْتَغْنَىٰ ۝٥ فَأَنتَ لَهُ تَصَدَّىٰ ۝٦ وَمَا عَلَيْكَ أَلَّا يَزَّكَّىٰ ۝٧ وَأَمَّا مَن جَاءَكَ يَسْعَىٰ ۝٨ وَهُوَ يَخْشَىٰ ۝٩ فَأَنتَ عَنْهُ تَلَهَّىٰ ۝١٠ كَلَّا إِنَّهَا تَذْكِرَةٌ ۝١١ فَمَن شَاءَ ذَكَرَهُ ۝١٢ فِي صُحُفٍ مُّكَرَّمَةٍ ۝١٣ مَّرْفُوعَةٍ مُّطَهَّرَةٍ ۝١٤ بِأَيْدِي سَفَرَةٍ ۝١٥ كِرَامٍ بَرَرَةٍ ۝١٦ قُتِلَ الْإِنسَانُ مَا أَكْفَرَهُ ۝١٧ مِنْ أَيِّ شَيْءٍ خَلَقَهُ ۝١٨ مِن نُّطْفَةٍ خَلَقَهُ فَقَدَّرَهُ ۝١٩ ثُمَّ السَّبِيلَ يَسَّرَهُ ۝٢٠ ثُمَّ أَمَاتَهُ فَأَقْبَرَهُ ۝٢١ ثُمَّ إِذَا شَاءَ أَنشَرَهُ ۝٢٢ كَلَّا لَمَّا يَقْضِ مَا أَمَرَهُ ۝٢٣ فَلْيَنظُرِ الْإِنسَانُ إِلَىٰ طَعَامِهِ ۝٢٤ أَنَّا صَبَبْنَا الْمَاءَ صَبًّا ۝٢٥ ثُمَّ شَقَقْنَا الْأَرْضَ شَقًّا ۝٢٦ فَأَنبَتْنَا فِيهَا حَبًّا ۝٢٧ وَعِنَبًا وَقَضْبًا ۝٢٨ وَزَيْتُونًا وَنَخْلًا ۝٢٩ وَحَدَائِقَ غُلْبًا ۝٣٠ وَفَاكِهَةً وَأَبًّا ۝٣١ مَّتَاعًا لَّكُمْ وَلِأَنْعَامِكُمْ ۝٣٢ فَإِذَا جَاءَتِ الصَّاخَّةُ ۝٣٣ يَوْمَ يَفِرُّ الْمَرْءُ مِنْ أَخِيهِ ۝٣٤ وَأُمِّهِ وَأَبِيهِ ۝٣٥ وَصَاحِبَتِهِ وَبَنِيهِ ۝٣٦ لِكُلِّ امْرِئٍ مِّنْهُمْ يَوْمَئِذٍ شَأْنٌ يُغْنِيهِ ۝٣٧ وُجُوهٌ يَوْمَئِذٍ مُّسْفِرَةٌ ۝٣٨ ضَاحِكَةٌ مُّسْتَبْشِرَةٌ ۝٣٩ وَوُجُوهٌ يَوْمَئِذٍ عَلَيْهَا غَبَرَةٌ ۝٤٠

My Juz' 'Amma Journey

Write down as many examples as you can from the page:

Identify Makharij of 6 letters	Ghunnah	Madd	Elevated sounds
------------------------------	-------	----	---------------
------------------------------	-------	----	---------------
------------------------------	-------	----	---------------
------------------------------	-------	----	---------------
------------------------------	-------	----	---------------

Noon Saakin & Tanween	Meem Saakin	Qalqalah	Hamzatul-wasl
Idgham: ------------------	Idgham: ------------	------------	------------
Ikhfaa': ------------------	Ikhfaa': ------------	------------	------------
Iqlab: ------------------			

الجزء الثلاثون — سُورَةُ عَبَسَ

بِسْمِ اللَّهِ الرَّحْمَنِ الرَّحِيمِ

عَبَسَ وَتَوَلَّىٰ ۝١ أَن جَاءَهُ الْأَعْمَىٰ ۝٢ وَمَا يُدْرِيكَ لَعَلَّهُ يَزَّكَّىٰ ۝٣ أَوْ يَذَّكَّرُ فَتَنفَعَهُ الذِّكْرَىٰ ۝٤ أَمَّا مَنِ اسْتَغْنَىٰ ۝٥ فَأَنتَ لَهُ تَصَدَّىٰ ۝٦ وَمَا عَلَيْكَ أَلَّا يَزَّكَّىٰ ۝٧ وَأَمَّا مَن جَاءَكَ يَسْعَىٰ ۝٨ وَهُوَ يَخْشَىٰ ۝٩ فَأَنتَ عَنْهُ تَلَهَّىٰ ۝١٠ كَلَّا إِنَّهَا تَذْكِرَةٌ ۝١١ فَمَن شَاءَ ذَكَرَهُ ۝١٢ فِي صُحُفٍ مُّكَرَّمَةٍ ۝١٣ مَّرْفُوعَةٍ مُّطَهَّرَةٍ ۝١٤ بِأَيْدِي سَفَرَةٍ ۝١٥ كِرَامٍ بَرَرَةٍ ۝١٦ قُتِلَ الْإِنسَانُ مَا أَكْفَرَهُ ۝١٧ مِنْ أَيِّ شَيْءٍ خَلَقَهُ ۝١٨ مِن نُّطْفَةٍ خَلَقَهُ فَقَدَّرَهُ ۝١٩ ثُمَّ السَّبِيلَ يَسَّرَهُ ۝٢٠ ثُمَّ أَمَاتَهُ فَأَقْبَرَهُ ۝٢١ ثُمَّ إِذَا شَاءَ أَنشَرَهُ ۝٢٢ كَلَّا لَمَّا يَقْضِ مَا أَمَرَهُ ۝٢٣ فَلْيَنظُرِ الْإِنسَانُ إِلَىٰ طَعَامِهِ ۝٢٤ أَنَّا صَبَبْنَا الْمَاءَ صَبًّا ۝٢٥ ثُمَّ شَقَقْنَا الْأَرْضَ شَقًّا ۝٢٦ فَأَنبَتْنَا فِيهَا حَبًّا ۝٢٧ وَعِنَبًا وَقَضْبًا ۝٢٨ وَزَيْتُونًا وَنَخْلًا ۝٢٩ وَحَدَائِقَ غُلْبًا ۝٣٠ وَفَاكِهَةً وَأَبًّا ۝٣١ مَّتَاعًا لَّكُمْ وَلِأَنْعَامِكُمْ ۝٣٢ فَإِذَا جَاءَتِ الصَّاخَّةُ ۝٣٣ يَوْمَ يَفِرُّ الْمَرْءُ مِنْ أَخِيهِ ۝٣٤ وَأُمِّهِ وَأَبِيهِ ۝٣٥ وَصَاحِبَتِهِ وَبَنِيهِ ۝٣٦ لِكُلِّ امْرِئٍ مِّنْهُمْ يَوْمَئِذٍ شَأْنٌ يُغْنِيهِ ۝٣٧ وُجُوهٌ يَوْمَئِذٍ مُّسْفِرَةٌ ۝٣٨ ضَاحِكَةٌ مُّسْتَبْشِرَةٌ ۝٣٩ وَوُجُوهٌ يَوْمَئِذٍ عَلَيْهَا غَبَرَةٌ ۝٤٠

٥٨٥

My Juz' 'Amma Journey

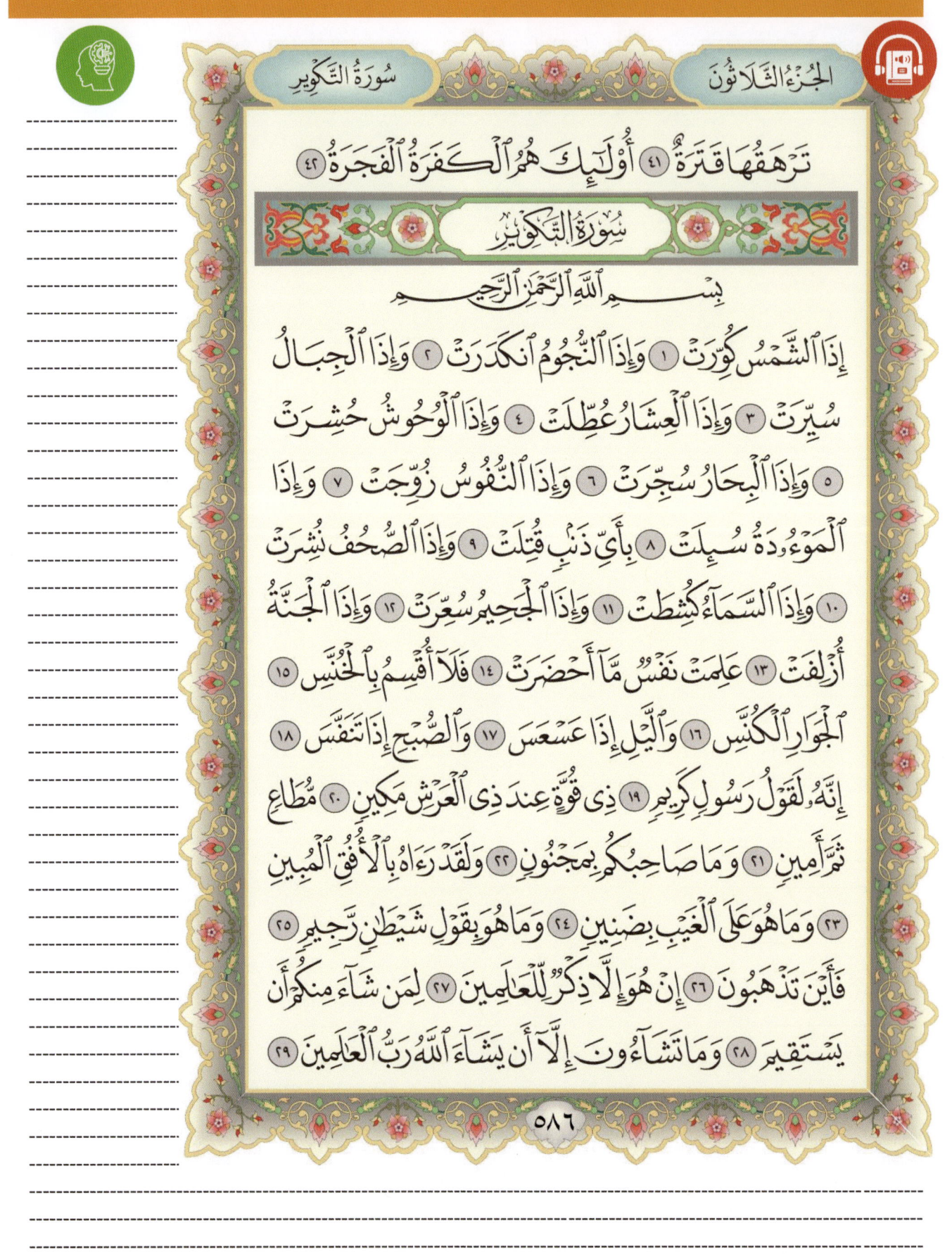

الجزء الثلاثون — سورة التكوير

تَرْهَقُهَا قَتَرَةٌ ۝٤١ أُولَٰئِكَ هُمُ الْكَفَرَةُ الْفَجَرَةُ ۝٤٢

سُورَةُ التَّكْوِيرِ

بِسْمِ اللَّهِ الرَّحْمَٰنِ الرَّحِيمِ

إِذَا الشَّمْسُ كُوِّرَتْ ۝١ وَإِذَا النُّجُومُ انكَدَرَتْ ۝٢ وَإِذَا الْجِبَالُ سُيِّرَتْ ۝٣ وَإِذَا الْعِشَارُ عُطِّلَتْ ۝٤ وَإِذَا الْوُحُوشُ حُشِرَتْ ۝٥ وَإِذَا الْبِحَارُ سُجِّرَتْ ۝٦ وَإِذَا النُّفُوسُ زُوِّجَتْ ۝٧ وَإِذَا الْمَوْءُودَةُ سُئِلَتْ ۝٨ بِأَيِّ ذَنبٍ قُتِلَتْ ۝٩ وَإِذَا الصُّحُفُ نُشِرَتْ ۝١٠ وَإِذَا السَّمَاءُ كُشِطَتْ ۝١١ وَإِذَا الْجَحِيمُ سُعِّرَتْ ۝١٢ وَإِذَا الْجَنَّةُ أُزْلِفَتْ ۝١٣ عَلِمَتْ نَفْسٌ مَّا أَحْضَرَتْ ۝١٤ فَلَا أُقْسِمُ بِالْخُنَّسِ ۝١٥ الْجَوَارِ الْكُنَّسِ ۝١٦ وَاللَّيْلِ إِذَا عَسْعَسَ ۝١٧ وَالصُّبْحِ إِذَا تَنَفَّسَ ۝١٨ إِنَّهُ لَقَوْلُ رَسُولٍ كَرِيمٍ ۝١٩ ذِي قُوَّةٍ عِندَ ذِي الْعَرْشِ مَكِينٍ ۝٢٠ مُّطَاعٍ ثَمَّ أَمِينٍ ۝٢١ وَمَا صَاحِبُكُم بِمَجْنُونٍ ۝٢٢ وَلَقَدْ رَآهُ بِالْأُفُقِ الْمُبِينِ ۝٢٣ وَمَا هُوَ عَلَى الْغَيْبِ بِضَنِينٍ ۝٢٤ وَمَا هُوَ بِقَوْلِ شَيْطَانٍ رَّجِيمٍ ۝٢٥ فَأَيْنَ تَذْهَبُونَ ۝٢٦ إِنْ هُوَ إِلَّا ذِكْرٌ لِّلْعَالَمِينَ ۝٢٧ لِمَن شَاءَ مِنكُمْ أَن يَسْتَقِيمَ ۝٢٨ وَمَا تَشَاءُونَ إِلَّا أَن يَشَاءَ اللَّهُ رَبُّ الْعَالَمِينَ ۝٢٩

٥٨٦

My Juz' 'Amma Journey

41, 42. Faces that will be extremely tired and humiliated. That will be the disbelievers' and wicked people's faces.

\multicolumn{4}{l}{Surah at-Takweer mentions the great changes that will happen before the Last Day.}
	1. When the sun shall be rolled round and lose its light,		2. And when the stars shall fall,
	3. And when the mountains shall perish,		4. And when the pregnant she-camels shall be neglected,
	5. And when the wild beasts shall be gathered,		6. And when the seas shall become as blazing Fire,
	7. And when the souls shall be joined with their bodies,		8 - 9. And when the female buried alive shall be questioned for what sin she was killed,
	10. And when the records of deeds of every person shall be opened,		11. And when the heaven shall be stripped off and taken away from its place,
	12. And when Hell-fire shall be kindled to fierce ablaze,		13. And when Paradise shall be brought near,
	14. Then every person will know what he has brought of good and evil.		15, 16. So, I swear by the planets that disappear during the day and appear during the night; moving swiftly,
	17. And by the night as it departs,		18. And by the dawn as it brightens,
	19. The Qur'an is Allah's speech that was conveyed by a trusted angel, Jibril.		20, 21. Owner of power, and high rank with Allah, the Lord of the Throne, obeyed by the angels and trustworthy in the heavens.
	22. O people, your companion Messenger is not a madman;		23. Indeed he saw Jibril in the clear horizon towards the east.
	24. And indeed he does not withhold knowledge of the unseen.		25. And the Qur'an is not the word of the outcast Satan.
	26. So, which path will you tread to deny that it is from Allah?		27. Verily, this Qur'an is no less than a Reminder to all.
	\multicolumn{3}{l}{28, 29. And it benefits whoever wills to be on the straight path. And whatever you will, Allah must will it first. He is the Lord of all.}

سُورَةُ التَّكْوِيرِ الجزءُ الثلاثونَ

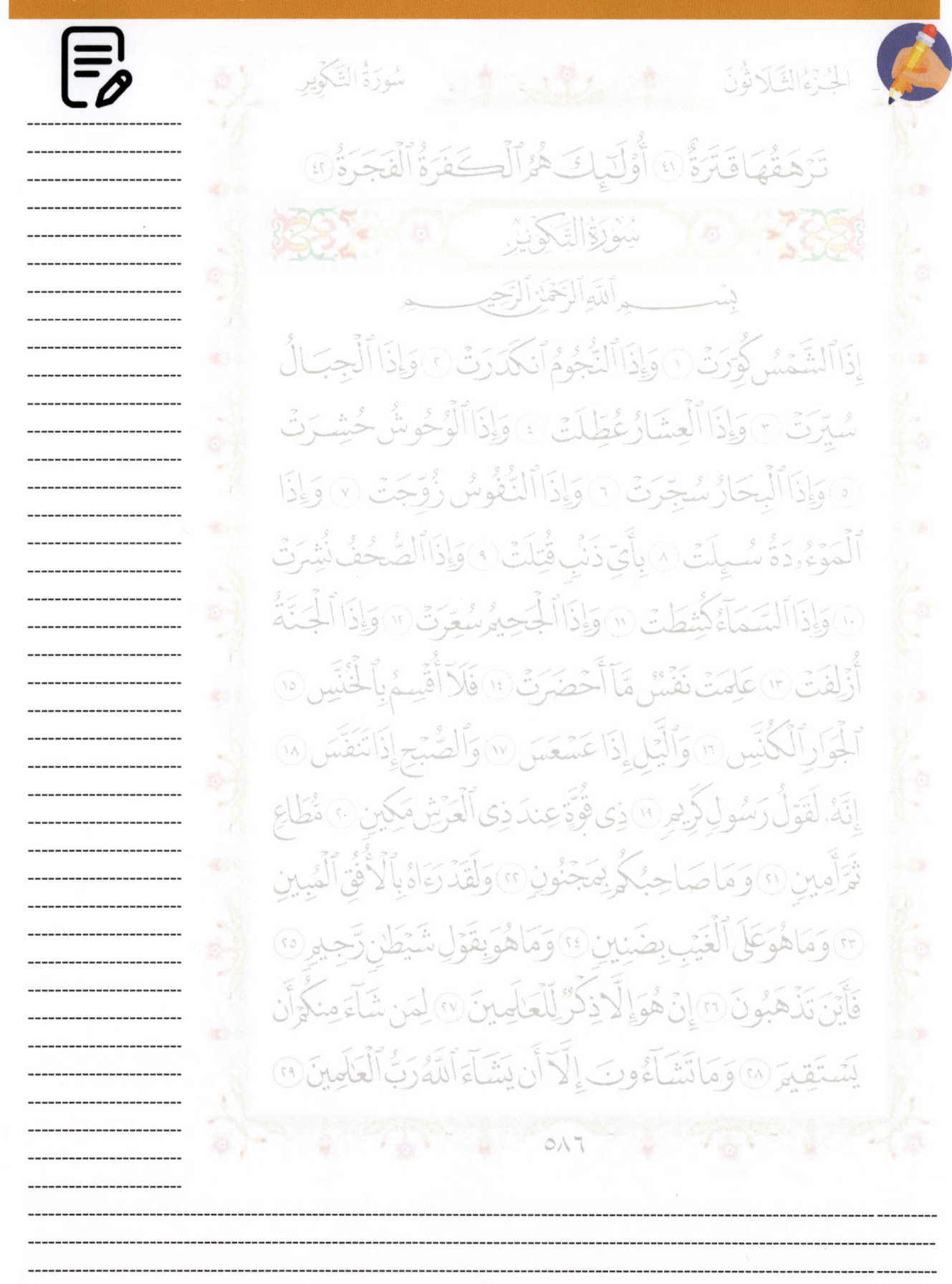

تَرْهَقُهَا قَتَرَةٌ ۝ أُوْلَٰٓئِكَ هُمُ ٱلْكَفَرَةُ ٱلْفَجَرَةُ ۝

سُورَةُ التَّكْوِيرِ

بِسْمِ ٱللَّهِ ٱلرَّحْمَٰنِ ٱلرَّحِيمِ

إِذَا ٱلشَّمْسُ كُوِّرَتْ ۝ وَإِذَا ٱلنُّجُومُ ٱنكَدَرَتْ ۝ وَإِذَا ٱلْجِبَالُ سُيِّرَتْ ۝ وَإِذَا ٱلْعِشَارُ عُطِّلَتْ ۝ وَإِذَا ٱلْوُحُوشُ حُشِرَتْ ۝ وَإِذَا ٱلْبِحَارُ سُجِّرَتْ ۝ وَإِذَا ٱلنُّفُوسُ زُوِّجَتْ ۝ وَإِذَا ٱلْمَوْءُۥدَةُ سُئِلَتْ ۝ بِأَيِّ ذَنۢبٍ قُتِلَتْ ۝ وَإِذَا ٱلصُّحُفُ نُشِرَتْ ۝ وَإِذَا ٱلسَّمَآءُ كُشِطَتْ ۝ وَإِذَا ٱلْجَحِيمُ سُعِّرَتْ ۝ وَإِذَا ٱلْجَنَّةُ أُزْلِفَتْ ۝ عَلِمَتْ نَفْسٌ مَّآ أَحْضَرَتْ ۝ فَلَآ أُقْسِمُ بِٱلْخُنَّسِ ۝ ٱلْجَوَارِ ٱلْكُنَّسِ ۝ وَٱلَّيْلِ إِذَا عَسْعَسَ ۝ وَٱلصُّبْحِ إِذَا تَنَفَّسَ ۝ إِنَّهُۥ لَقَوْلُ رَسُولٍ كَرِيمٍ ۝ ذِى قُوَّةٍ عِندَ ذِى ٱلْعَرْشِ مَكِينٍ ۝ مُّطَاعٍ ثَمَّ أَمِينٍ ۝ وَمَا صَاحِبُكُم بِمَجْنُونٍ ۝ وَلَقَدْ رَءَاهُ بِٱلْأُفُقِ ٱلْمُبِينِ ۝ وَمَا هُوَ عَلَى ٱلْغَيْبِ بِضَنِينٍ ۝ وَمَا هُوَ بِقَوْلِ شَيْطَٰنٍ رَّجِيمٍ ۝ فَأَيْنَ تَذْهَبُونَ ۝ إِنْ هُوَ إِلَّا ذِكْرٌ لِّلْعَٰلَمِينَ ۝ لِمَن شَآءَ مِنكُمْ أَن يَسْتَقِيمَ ۝ وَمَا تَشَآءُونَ إِلَّآ أَن يَشَآءَ ٱللَّهُ رَبُّ ٱلْعَٰلَمِينَ ۝

٥٨٦

My Juz' 'Amma Journey

Write down as many examples as you can from the page:

Identify Makharij of 6 letters	Ghunnah	Madd	Elevated sounds

Noon Saakin & Tanween	Meem Saakin	Qalqalah	Hamzatul-wasl
Idgham: ------------------- Ikhfaa': ------------------- Iqlab: -------------------	Idgham: ------------------- Ikhfaa': -------------------		

24

Surah al-Infitar portrays the resurrection through the scattering of creatures and the changing of their conditions.

1. When the heaven is split asunder,

2. And when the stars have fallen and scattered,

3. And when the seas are burst forth,

4. And when the graves are turned upside down and bring out their contents,

5. Then a person will know what he has sent forward and what he has left behind of good or bad deeds.

6-8. O man! What has made you careless concerning your Lord, the Most Generous, Who created you, fashioned you perfectly, and gave you due proportion? He could make you in whatever form He willed.

9. Nay! But you deny the Recompense.

10-12. But verily, over you are appointed honourable angels watching you and writing down your deeds. They know all that you do.

13. Verily, the pious and righteous will be in delight.

14-15. And verily on the Day of Recompense, the wicked will be in the blazing Fire, tasting its burning flame, and they will not go out from it.

17-19. Do you know what the Day of Recompense is? It will be the Day when no person shall have power to do anything for another, and the Decision, that Day, will be wholly with Allah.

Surah al-Mutafefin explains the different conditions of people in the scales and speaks about the next homes.

1-3. Woe to those who give less in measure and weight, decreasing the rights of others. When they receive by measure, they demand full measure. And when they give by measure, they give less than due.

4. Do they not think that they will be resurrected for reckoning?

سُورَةُ الِانْفِطَارِ

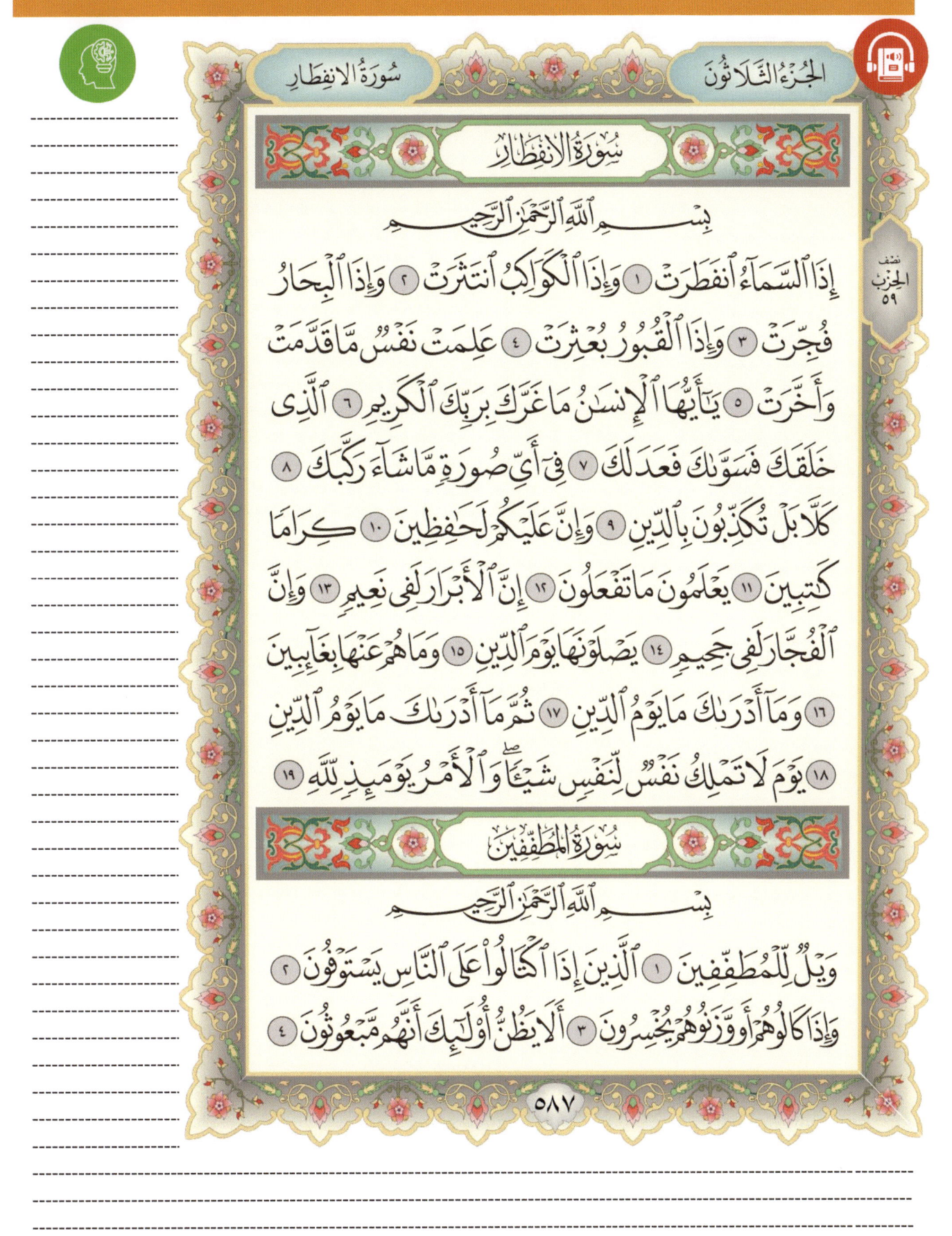

بِسْمِ اللَّهِ الرَّحْمَٰنِ الرَّحِيمِ

إِذَا السَّمَاءُ انْفَطَرَتْ ۝١ وَإِذَا الْكَوَاكِبُ انْتَثَرَتْ ۝٢ وَإِذَا الْبِحَارُ فُجِّرَتْ ۝٣ وَإِذَا الْقُبُورُ بُعْثِرَتْ ۝٤ عَلِمَتْ نَفْسٌ مَّا قَدَّمَتْ وَأَخَّرَتْ ۝٥ يَٰٓأَيُّهَا الْإِنسَٰنُ مَا غَرَّكَ بِرَبِّكَ الْكَرِيمِ ۝٦ الَّذِى خَلَقَكَ فَسَوَّىٰكَ فَعَدَلَكَ ۝٧ فِىٓ أَىِّ صُورَةٍ مَّا شَآءَ رَكَّبَكَ ۝٨ كَلَّا بَلْ تُكَذِّبُونَ بِالدِّينِ ۝٩ وَإِنَّ عَلَيْكُمْ لَحَٰفِظِينَ ۝١٠ كِرَامًا كَٰتِبِينَ ۝١١ يَعْلَمُونَ مَا تَفْعَلُونَ ۝١٢ إِنَّ الْأَبْرَارَ لَفِى نَعِيمٍ ۝١٣ وَإِنَّ الْفُجَّارَ لَفِى جَحِيمٍ ۝١٤ يَصْلَوْنَهَا يَوْمَ الدِّينِ ۝١٥ وَمَا هُمْ عَنْهَا بِغَآئِبِينَ ۝١٦ وَمَآ أَدْرَىٰكَ مَا يَوْمُ الدِّينِ ۝١٧ ثُمَّ مَآ أَدْرَىٰكَ مَا يَوْمُ الدِّينِ ۝١٨ يَوْمَ لَا تَمْلِكُ نَفْسٌ لِّنَفْسٍ شَيْـًٔا ۖ وَالْأَمْرُ يَوْمَئِذٍ لِّلَّهِ ۝١٩

سُورَةُ الْمُطَفِّفِينَ

بِسْمِ اللَّهِ الرَّحْمَٰنِ الرَّحِيمِ

وَيْلٌ لِّلْمُطَفِّفِينَ ۝١ الَّذِينَ إِذَا اكْتَالُوا عَلَى النَّاسِ يَسْتَوْفُونَ ۝٢ وَإِذَا كَالُوهُمْ أَو وَّزَنُوهُمْ يُخْسِرُونَ ۝٣ أَلَا يَظُنُّ أُولَٰٓئِكَ أَنَّهُم مَّبْعُوثُونَ ۝٤

My Juz' 'Amma Journey

Write down as many examples as you can from the page:

Identify Makharij of 6 letters	Ghunnah	Madd	Elevated sounds

Noon Saakin & Tanween	Meem Saakin	Qalqalah	Hamzatul-wasl
Idgham: _____ Ikhfaa': _____ Iqlab: _____	Idgham: _____ Ikhfaa': _____		

الجزء الثلاثون ۞ سورة الانفطار

سورة الانفطار

بِسْمِ اللَّهِ الرَّحْمَٰنِ الرَّحِيمِ

إِذَا السَّمَاءُ انْفَطَرَتْ ۝ وَإِذَا الْكَوَاكِبُ انْتَثَرَتْ ۝ وَإِذَا الْبِحَارُ فُجِّرَتْ ۝ وَإِذَا الْقُبُورُ بُعْثِرَتْ ۝ عَلِمَتْ نَفْسٌ مَا قَدَّمَتْ وَأَخَّرَتْ ۝ يَا أَيُّهَا الْإِنْسَانُ مَا غَرَّكَ بِرَبِّكَ الْكَرِيمِ ۝ الَّذِي خَلَقَكَ فَسَوَّاكَ فَعَدَلَكَ ۝ فِي أَيِّ صُورَةٍ مَا شَاءَ رَكَّبَكَ ۝ كَلَّا بَلْ تُكَذِّبُونَ بِالدِّينِ ۝ وَإِنَّ عَلَيْكُمْ لَحَافِظِينَ ۝ كِرَامًا كَاتِبِينَ ۝ يَعْلَمُونَ مَا تَفْعَلُونَ ۝ إِنَّ الْأَبْرَارَ لَفِي نَعِيمٍ ۝ وَإِنَّ الْفُجَّارَ لَفِي جَحِيمٍ ۝ يَصْلَوْنَهَا يَوْمَ الدِّينِ ۝ وَمَا هُمْ عَنْهَا بِغَائِبِينَ ۝ وَمَا أَدْرَاكَ مَا يَوْمُ الدِّينِ ۝ ثُمَّ مَا أَدْرَاكَ مَا يَوْمُ الدِّينِ ۝ يَوْمَ لَا تَمْلِكُ نَفْسٌ لِنَفْسٍ شَيْئًا وَالْأَمْرُ يَوْمَئِذٍ لِلَّهِ ۝

سورة المطففين

بِسْمِ اللَّهِ الرَّحْمَٰنِ الرَّحِيمِ

وَيْلٌ لِلْمُطَفِّفِينَ ۝ الَّذِينَ إِذَا اكْتَالُوا عَلَى النَّاسِ يَسْتَوْفُونَ ۝ وَإِذَا كَالُوهُمْ أَوْ وَزَنُوهُمْ يُخْسِرُونَ ۝ أَلَا يَظُنُّ أُولَٰئِكَ أَنَّهُمْ مَبْعُوثُونَ ۝

٥٨٧

الجزء الثلاثون — سورة المطففين

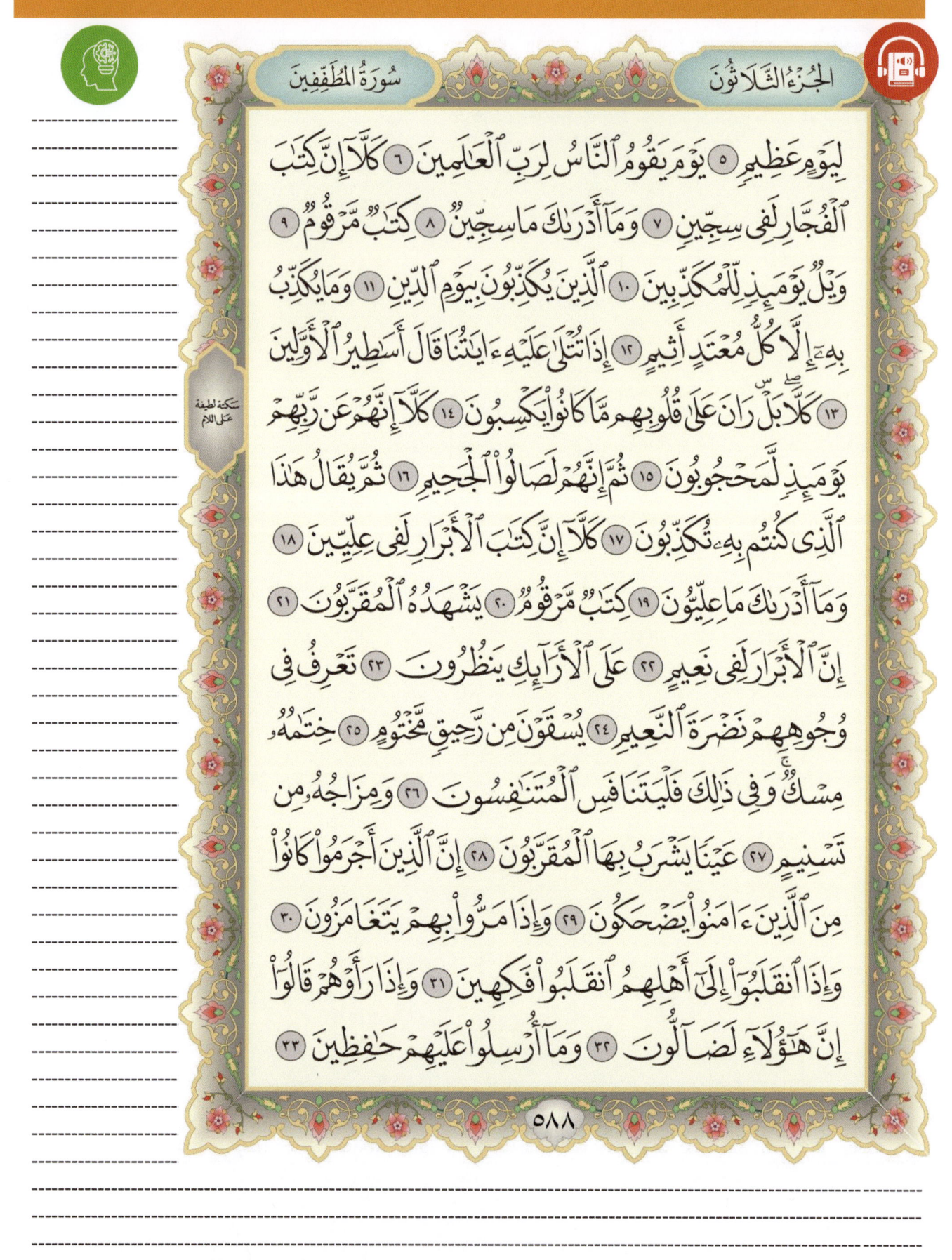

لِيَوْمٍ عَظِيمٍ ۝ يَوْمَ يَقُومُ النَّاسُ لِرَبِّ الْعَالَمِينَ ۝ كَلَّا إِنَّ كِتَابَ الْفُجَّارِ لَفِي سِجِّينٍ ۝ وَمَا أَدْرَاكَ مَا سِجِّينٌ ۝ كِتَابٌ مَّرْقُومٌ ۝ وَيْلٌ يَوْمَئِذٍ لِّلْمُكَذِّبِينَ ۝ الَّذِينَ يُكَذِّبُونَ بِيَوْمِ الدِّينِ ۝ وَمَا يُكَذِّبُ بِهِ إِلَّا كُلُّ مُعْتَدٍ أَثِيمٍ ۝ إِذَا تُتْلَىٰ عَلَيْهِ آيَاتُنَا قَالَ أَسَاطِيرُ الْأَوَّلِينَ ۝ كَلَّا ۖ بَلْ ۜ رَانَ عَلَىٰ قُلُوبِهِم مَّا كَانُوا يَكْسِبُونَ ۝ كَلَّا إِنَّهُمْ عَن رَّبِّهِمْ يَوْمَئِذٍ لَّمَحْجُوبُونَ ۝ ثُمَّ إِنَّهُمْ لَصَالُوا الْجَحِيمِ ۝ ثُمَّ يُقَالُ هَٰذَا الَّذِي كُنتُم بِهِ تُكَذِّبُونَ ۝ كَلَّا إِنَّ كِتَابَ الْأَبْرَارِ لَفِي عِلِّيِّينَ ۝ وَمَا أَدْرَاكَ مَا عِلِّيُّونَ ۝ كِتَابٌ مَّرْقُومٌ ۝ يَشْهَدُهُ الْمُقَرَّبُونَ ۝ إِنَّ الْأَبْرَارَ لَفِي نَعِيمٍ ۝ عَلَى الْأَرَائِكِ يَنظُرُونَ ۝ تَعْرِفُ فِي وُجُوهِهِمْ نَضْرَةَ النَّعِيمِ ۝ يُسْقَوْنَ مِن رَّحِيقٍ مَّخْتُومٍ ۝ خِتَامُهُ مِسْكٌ ۚ وَفِي ذَٰلِكَ فَلْيَتَنَافَسِ الْمُتَنَافِسُونَ ۝ وَمِزَاجُهُ مِن تَسْنِيمٍ ۝ عَيْنًا يَشْرَبُ بِهَا الْمُقَرَّبُونَ ۝ إِنَّ الَّذِينَ أَجْرَمُوا كَانُوا مِنَ الَّذِينَ آمَنُوا يَضْحَكُونَ ۝ وَإِذَا مَرُّوا بِهِمْ يَتَغَامَزُونَ ۝ وَإِذَا انقَلَبُوا إِلَىٰ أَهْلِهِمُ انقَلَبُوا فَكِهِينَ ۝ وَإِذَا رَأَوْهُمْ قَالُوا إِنَّ هَٰؤُلَاءِ لَضَالُّونَ ۝ وَمَا أُرْسِلُوا عَلَيْهِمْ حَافِظِينَ ۝

٥٨٨

	5, 6. Don't they know that they will be resurrected on a Great Day, when all mankind will stand before the Lord of the worlds?
	7-9. Nay! Truly, the record of the deeds of the wicked is preserved in Sijjin taking them down to the Hell. Do you know what Sijjin is? It is an inscribed Register.
	10-13. Woe, that Day, to those who deny the Day of Recompense. And none can deny it except every transgressor. When Our verses are recited to him, he says: "Tales of the ancients!"
	14-17. Nay! But on their hearts is the covering of sins which they used to earn. Surely, the evil doers will be veiled from seeing their Lord that Day. Then, they will indeed enter and taste the burning flame of Hell. Then, it will be said to them: "This is what you used to deny!"
	18-21. Verily, the Record of the deeds of the pious is preserved in 'Illiyyun taking them up to the Heaven. Do you know what 'Illiyyun is? It is an inscribed Register. To which bear witness the angels, those nearest to Allah.
	22-24. Verily, the pious will be in delight, on thrones looking at what pleases them. You will recognise in their faces the brightness of delight.
	25-28. They will be given to drink pure sealed wine, the last bit of which will be musk; and for this let the competitors compete. That wine will be mixed with Tasneem, a spring from which those nearest to Allah will drink.
	29. Indeed, during the worldly life, the wicked people used to laugh at those who believed.
	30. And whenever they passed by them, they used to wink to one another in mockery.
	31-33. And when they returned to their own people, they would return jesting. And when they saw them, they said: "These people have indeed gone astray!" However, they had not been sent as watchers over them.

سورة المطففين الجزء الثلاثون

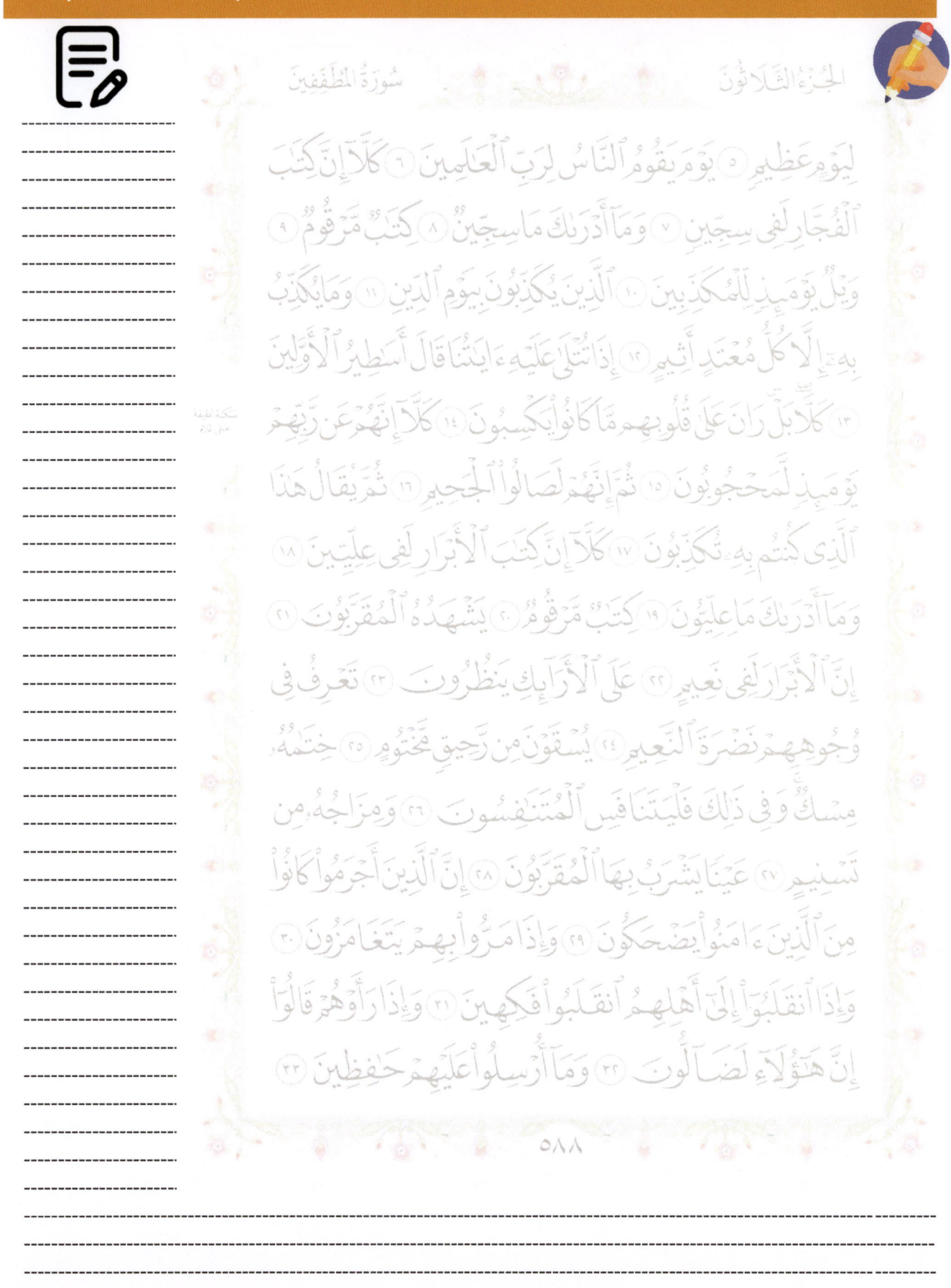

لِيَوْمٍ عَظِيمٍ ۝ يَوْمَ يَقُومُ ٱلنَّاسُ لِرَبِّ ٱلْعَٰلَمِينَ ۝ كَلَّآ إِنَّ كِتَٰبَ ٱلْفُجَّارِ لَفِى سِجِّينٍ ۝ وَمَآ أَدْرَىٰكَ مَا سِجِّينٌ ۝ كِتَٰبٌ مَّرْقُومٌ ۝ وَيْلٌ يَوْمَئِذٍ لِّلْمُكَذِّبِينَ ۝ ٱلَّذِينَ يُكَذِّبُونَ بِيَوْمِ ٱلدِّينِ ۝ وَمَا يُكَذِّبُ بِهِۦٓ إِلَّا كُلُّ مُعْتَدٍ أَثِيمٍ ۝ إِذَا تُتْلَىٰ عَلَيْهِ ءَايَٰتُنَا قَالَ أَسَٰطِيرُ ٱلْأَوَّلِينَ ۝ كَلَّا ۖ بَلْ ۜ رَانَ عَلَىٰ قُلُوبِهِم مَّا كَانُوا۟ يَكْسِبُونَ ۝ كَلَّآ إِنَّهُمْ عَن رَّبِّهِمْ يَوْمَئِذٍ لَّمَحْجُوبُونَ ۝ ثُمَّ إِنَّهُمْ لَصَالُوا۟ ٱلْجَحِيمِ ۝ ثُمَّ يُقَالُ هَٰذَا ٱلَّذِى كُنتُم بِهِۦ تُكَذِّبُونَ ۝ كَلَّآ إِنَّ كِتَٰبَ ٱلْأَبْرَارِ لَفِى عِلِّيِّينَ ۝ وَمَآ أَدْرَىٰكَ مَا عِلِّيُّونَ ۝ كِتَٰبٌ مَّرْقُومٌ ۝ يَشْهَدُهُ ٱلْمُقَرَّبُونَ ۝ إِنَّ ٱلْأَبْرَارَ لَفِى نَعِيمٍ ۝ عَلَى ٱلْأَرَآئِكِ يَنظُرُونَ ۝ تَعْرِفُ فِى وُجُوهِهِمْ نَضْرَةَ ٱلنَّعِيمِ ۝ يُسْقَوْنَ مِن رَّحِيقٍ مَّخْتُومٍ ۝ خِتَٰمُهُۥ مِسْكٌ ۚ وَفِى ذَٰلِكَ فَلْيَتَنَافَسِ ٱلْمُتَنَٰفِسُونَ ۝ وَمِزَاجُهُۥ مِن تَسْنِيمٍ ۝ عَيْنًا يَشْرَبُ بِهَا ٱلْمُقَرَّبُونَ ۝ إِنَّ ٱلَّذِينَ أَجْرَمُوا۟ كَانُوا۟ مِنَ ٱلَّذِينَ ءَامَنُوا۟ يَضْحَكُونَ ۝ وَإِذَا مَرُّوا۟ بِهِمْ يَتَغَامَزُونَ ۝ وَإِذَا ٱنقَلَبُوٓا۟ إِلَىٰٓ أَهْلِهِمُ ٱنقَلَبُوا۟ فَكِهِينَ ۝ وَإِذَا رَأَوْهُمْ قَالُوٓا۟ إِنَّ هَٰٓؤُلَآءِ لَضَآلُّونَ ۝ وَمَآ أُرْسِلُوا۟ عَلَيْهِمْ حَٰفِظِينَ ۝

٥٨٨

My Juz' 'Amma Journey

Write down as many examples as you can from the page:

Identify Makharij of 6 letters	Ghunnah	Madd	Elevated sounds

Noon Saakin & Tanween	Meem Saakin	Qalqalah	Hamzatul-wasl
Idgham: —————— Ikhfaa': —————— Iqlab: ——————	Idgham: —————— Ikhfaa': ——————		

32

My Juz' 'Amma Journey

34, 35. But on that Day, those who believed will laugh at those who disbelieved whilst they will be on high thrones looking at what pleases them.

36. Do you not think that, by this, the disbelievers would pay fully for what they used to do?

Surah al-Inshiqaq portrays the whole universe surrendering to Allah in obedience.

1, 2. The hour will begin when the heaven is split asunder and listens and obeys its Lord, and it must do so.

3-5. And when the earth is stretched forth and has cast out all that was in it and became empty, and listens and obeys its Lord, and it must do so.

6. O man! Verily, you are surely returning to your Lord with your deeds, so you will meet Him to receive your reward or punishment.

7-9. Then, as for him who will be given his record in his right hand, he surely will receive an easy reckoning and will return to his family in joy.

10-15. But he who is given his record behind his back, he will invoke his destruction, and shall enter a blazing Fire, and taste its burning. Verily, he was among his people in joy thinking that he would never come back to Us! Indeed, his Lord has been ever observing him.

16-19. So, I swear by the afterglow of sunset, by the night and whatever it gathers in its darkness, and by the moon when it is at the full; you shall certainly go through stage after stage in this life and in the Hereafter.

20, 21. What is the matter with the disbeliever that they do not believe, and when the Qur'an is recited to them, they do not fall prostrate?

22. This is because they belie the Qur'an and the truth.

23, 24. And Allah knows best what is in their hearts. So, proclaim to them a painful torment.

الجزء الثلاثون — سُورَةُ الانشقاق

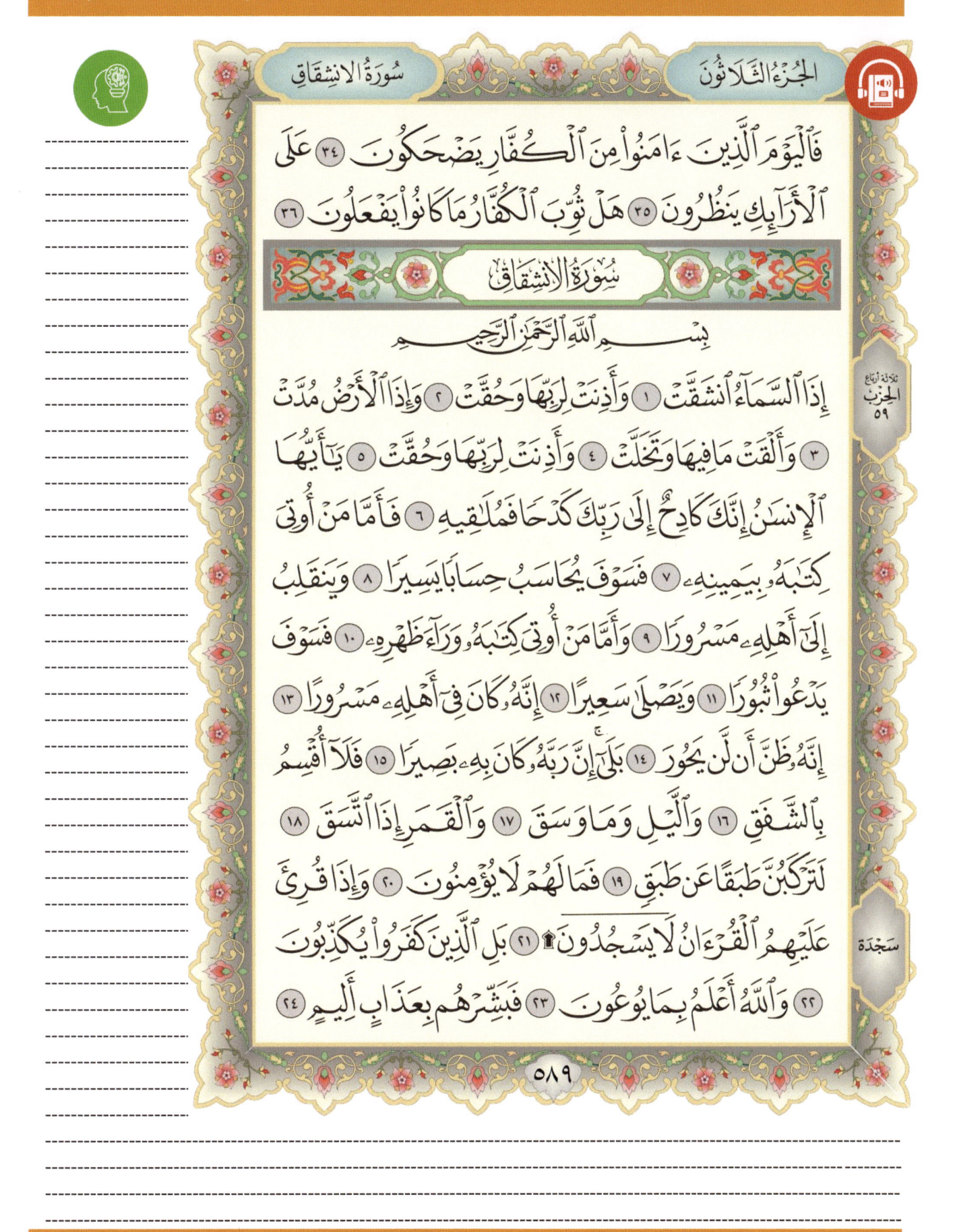

فَالْيَوْمَ الَّذِينَ ءَامَنُوا مِنَ الْكُفَّارِ يَضْحَكُونَ ۝٣٤ عَلَى الْأَرَآئِكِ يَنظُرُونَ ۝٣٥ هَلْ ثُوِّبَ الْكُفَّارُ مَا كَانُوا يَفْعَلُونَ ۝٣٦

سُورَةُ الانشقاق

بِسْمِ اللَّهِ الرَّحْمَٰنِ الرَّحِيمِ

إِذَا السَّمَآءُ انشَقَّتْ ۝١ وَأَذِنَتْ لِرَبِّهَا وَحُقَّتْ ۝٢ وَإِذَا الْأَرْضُ مُدَّتْ ۝٣ وَأَلْقَتْ مَا فِيهَا وَتَخَلَّتْ ۝٤ وَأَذِنَتْ لِرَبِّهَا وَحُقَّتْ ۝٥ يَٰٓأَيُّهَا الْإِنسَٰنُ إِنَّكَ كَادِحٌ إِلَىٰ رَبِّكَ كَدْحًا فَمُلَٰقِيهِ ۝٦ فَأَمَّا مَنْ أُوتِىَ كِتَٰبَهُۥ بِيَمِينِهِۦ ۝٧ فَسَوْفَ يُحَاسَبُ حِسَابًا يَسِيرًا ۝٨ وَيَنقَلِبُ إِلَىٰٓ أَهْلِهِۦ مَسْرُورًا ۝٩ وَأَمَّا مَنْ أُوتِىَ كِتَٰبَهُۥ وَرَآءَ ظَهْرِهِۦ ۝١٠ فَسَوْفَ يَدْعُوا ثُبُورًا ۝١١ وَيَصْلَىٰ سَعِيرًا ۝١٢ إِنَّهُۥ كَانَ فِىٓ أَهْلِهِۦ مَسْرُورًا ۝١٣ إِنَّهُۥ ظَنَّ أَن لَّن يَحُورَ ۝١٤ بَلَىٰٓ إِنَّ رَبَّهُۥ كَانَ بِهِۦ بَصِيرًا ۝١٥ فَلَآ أُقْسِمُ بِالشَّفَقِ ۝١٦ وَالَّيْلِ وَمَا وَسَقَ ۝١٧ وَالْقَمَرِ إِذَا اتَّسَقَ ۝١٨ لَتَرْكَبُنَّ طَبَقًا عَن طَبَقٍ ۝١٩ فَمَا لَهُمْ لَا يُؤْمِنُونَ ۝٢٠ وَإِذَا قُرِئَ عَلَيْهِمُ الْقُرْءَانُ لَا يَسْجُدُونَ ۩ ۝٢١ بَلِ الَّذِينَ كَفَرُوا يُكَذِّبُونَ ۝٢٢ وَاللَّهُ أَعْلَمُ بِمَا يُوعُونَ ۝٢٣ فَبَشِّرْهُم بِعَذَابٍ أَلِيمٍ ۝٢٤

٥٨٩

My Juz' 'Amma Journey

Write down as many examples as you can from the page:

Identify Makharij of 6 letters	Ghunnah	Madd	Elevated sounds

Noon Saakin & Tanween	Meem Saakin	Qalqalah	Hamzatul-wasl
Idgham: ——————	Idgham: ——————	——————	——————
Ikhfaa': ——————	Ikhfaa': ——————		
Iqlab: ——————			

سورة الانشقاق

الجزء الثلاثون

فَالْيَوْمَ الَّذِينَ ءَامَنُوا مِنَ الْكُفَّارِ يَضْحَكُونَ ۝ عَلَى الْأَرَائِكِ يَنظُرُونَ ۝ هَلْ ثُوِّبَ الْكُفَّارُ مَا كَانُوا يَفْعَلُونَ ۝

سورة الانشقاق

بِسْمِ اللَّهِ الرَّحْمَٰنِ الرَّحِيمِ

إِذَا السَّمَاءُ انشَقَّتْ ۝ وَأَذِنَتْ لِرَبِّهَا وَحُقَّتْ ۝ وَإِذَا الْأَرْضُ مُدَّتْ ۝ وَأَلْقَتْ مَا فِيهَا وَتَخَلَّتْ ۝ وَأَذِنَتْ لِرَبِّهَا وَحُقَّتْ ۝ يَا أَيُّهَا الْإِنسَانُ إِنَّكَ كَادِحٌ إِلَىٰ رَبِّكَ كَدْحًا فَمُلَاقِيهِ ۝ فَأَمَّا مَنْ أُوتِيَ كِتَابَهُ بِيَمِينِهِ ۝ فَسَوْفَ يُحَاسَبُ حِسَابًا يَسِيرًا ۝ وَيَنقَلِبُ إِلَىٰ أَهْلِهِ مَسْرُورًا ۝ وَأَمَّا مَنْ أُوتِيَ كِتَابَهُ وَرَاءَ ظَهْرِهِ ۝ فَسَوْفَ يَدْعُو ثُبُورًا ۝ وَيَصْلَىٰ سَعِيرًا ۝ إِنَّهُ كَانَ فِي أَهْلِهِ مَسْرُورًا ۝ إِنَّهُ ظَنَّ أَن لَّن يَحُورَ ۝ بَلَىٰ إِنَّ رَبَّهُ كَانَ بِهِ بَصِيرًا ۝ فَلَا أُقْسِمُ بِالشَّفَقِ ۝ وَاللَّيْلِ وَمَا وَسَقَ ۝ وَالْقَمَرِ إِذَا اتَّسَقَ ۝ لَتَرْكَبُنَّ طَبَقًا عَن طَبَقٍ ۝ فَمَا لَهُمْ لَا يُؤْمِنُونَ ۝ وَإِذَا قُرِئَ عَلَيْهِمُ الْقُرْآنُ لَا يَسْجُدُونَ ۩ ۝ بَلِ الَّذِينَ كَفَرُوا يُكَذِّبُونَ ۝ وَاللَّهُ أَعْلَمُ بِمَا يُوعُونَ ۝ فَبَشِّرْهُم بِعَذَابٍ أَلِيمٍ ۝

٥٨٩

سُورَةُ الْبُرُوجِ

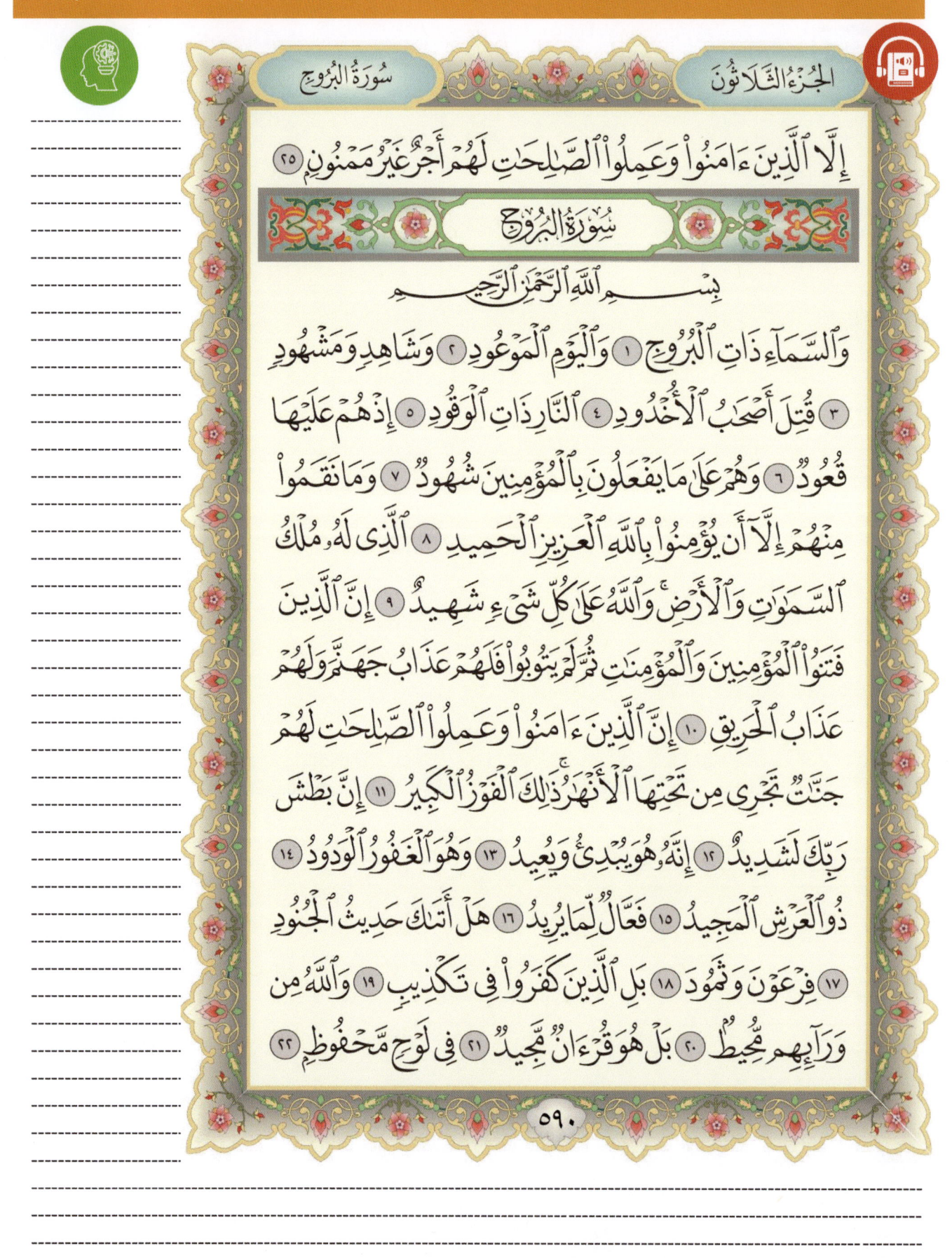

إِلَّا الَّذِينَ ءَامَنُوا۟ وَعَمِلُوا۟ الصَّـٰلِحَـٰتِ لَهُمْ أَجْرٌ غَيْرُ مَمْنُونٍ ۝٢٥

سُورَةُ الْبُرُوجِ

بِسْمِ اللَّهِ الرَّحْمَـٰنِ الرَّحِيمِ

وَالسَّمَآءِ ذَاتِ الْبُرُوجِ ۝١ وَالْيَوْمِ الْمَوْعُودِ ۝٢ وَشَاهِدٍ وَمَشْهُودٍ ۝٣ قُتِلَ أَصْحَـٰبُ الْأُخْدُودِ ۝٤ النَّارِ ذَاتِ الْوَقُودِ ۝٥ إِذْ هُمْ عَلَيْهَا قُعُودٌ ۝٦ وَهُمْ عَلَىٰ مَا يَفْعَلُونَ بِالْمُؤْمِنِينَ شُهُودٌ ۝٧ وَمَا نَقَمُوا۟ مِنْهُمْ إِلَّآ أَن يُؤْمِنُوا۟ بِاللَّهِ الْعَزِيزِ الْحَمِيدِ ۝٨ الَّذِى لَهُۥ مُلْكُ السَّمَـٰوَٰتِ وَالْأَرْضِ ۚ وَاللَّهُ عَلَىٰ كُلِّ شَىْءٍ شَهِيدٌ ۝٩ إِنَّ الَّذِينَ فَتَنُوا۟ الْمُؤْمِنِينَ وَالْمُؤْمِنَـٰتِ ثُمَّ لَمْ يَتُوبُوا۟ فَلَهُمْ عَذَابُ جَهَنَّمَ وَلَهُمْ عَذَابُ الْحَرِيقِ ۝١٠ إِنَّ الَّذِينَ ءَامَنُوا۟ وَعَمِلُوا۟ الصَّـٰلِحَـٰتِ لَهُمْ جَنَّـٰتٌ تَجْرِى مِن تَحْتِهَا الْأَنْهَـٰرُ ۚ ذَٰلِكَ الْفَوْزُ الْكَبِيرُ ۝١١ إِنَّ بَطْشَ رَبِّكَ لَشَدِيدٌ ۝١٢ إِنَّهُۥ هُوَ يُبْدِئُ وَيُعِيدُ ۝١٣ وَهُوَ الْغَفُورُ الْوَدُودُ ۝١٤ ذُو الْعَرْشِ الْمَجِيدُ ۝١٥ فَعَّالٌ لِّمَا يُرِيدُ ۝١٦ هَلْ أَتَىٰكَ حَدِيثُ الْجُنُودِ ۝١٧ فِرْعَوْنَ وَثَمُودَ ۝١٨ بَلِ الَّذِينَ كَفَرُوا۟ فِى تَكْذِيبٍ ۝١٩ وَاللَّهُ مِن وَرَآئِهِم مُّحِيطٌ ۝٢٠ بَلْ هُوَ قُرْءَانٌ مَّجِيدٌ ۝٢١ فِى لَوْحٍ مَّحْفُوظٍ ۝٢٢

٥٩٠

25. Except those who believe and do good deeds; for them is a reward in Paradise that will never come to an end.

Surah al-Burooj demonstrates Allah's Power and comprehensive Encompassment. It also threatens those who ambush the believers with severe punishment.

1. By the heaven, holding the big stars,

2. And by the Promised Day of Resurrection,

3. And by every witnessing, like a prophet testifying to his nation, and by every witnessed thing, like the day of 'Arafah,

4. Cursed were the people of the ditch.

5-7. When they set a fuelled fire in it, sat by it and threw the believers in it alive, witnessing what they were doing to them.

8, 9. They had nothing against them except that they believed in Allah the All-Mighty, Worthy of all Praise, to Whom belongs the dominion of the heavens and the earth! And Allah is the Witness over everything.

10. Verily, those who put the believing men and women into trial by torturing them, and then do not turn to Allah in repentance will have the torment of Hell where they will suffer the punishment of the burning Fire.

11. Verily, for those who believe and do good deeds there will be Gardens in Paradise under which rivers flow. That is the great success.

12-16. Verily, the Punishment of your Lord is severe, as He begins everything and repeats it. And He is Oft-Forgiving, full of love towards the pious, Owner of the throne and the Glorious. He does what He wills

17, 18. Has the story of the hosts of Fir'aun and Thamud reached you?

19, 20. The disbelievers persist in denying and Allah surrounds them and keeps a record of their actions.

21, 22. The Qur'an which they claim it to be poetry is, rather, a noble Qur'an inscribed in The Tablet Preserved under Allah's Throne.

My Juz' 'Amma Journey

الجزء الثلاثون   سُورَةُ البُرُوجِ

إِلَّا ٱلَّذِينَ ءَامَنُوا۟ وَعَمِلُوا۟ ٱلصَّٰلِحَٰتِ لَهُمْ أَجْرٌ غَيْرُ مَمْنُونٍۭ ۝٢٥

سُورَةُ البُرُوجِ

بِسْمِ ٱللَّهِ ٱلرَّحْمَٰنِ ٱلرَّحِيمِ

وَٱلسَّمَآءِ ذَاتِ ٱلْبُرُوجِ ۝١ وَٱلْيَوْمِ ٱلْمَوْعُودِ ۝٢ وَشَاهِدٍ وَمَشْهُودٍ ۝٣ قُتِلَ أَصْحَٰبُ ٱلْأُخْدُودِ ۝٤ ٱلنَّارِ ذَاتِ ٱلْوَقُودِ ۝٥ إِذْ هُمْ عَلَيْهَا قُعُودٌ ۝٦ وَهُمْ عَلَىٰ مَا يَفْعَلُونَ بِٱلْمُؤْمِنِينَ شُهُودٌ ۝٧ وَمَا نَقَمُوا۟ مِنْهُمْ إِلَّآ أَن يُؤْمِنُوا۟ بِٱللَّهِ ٱلْعَزِيزِ ٱلْحَمِيدِ ۝٨ ٱلَّذِى لَهُۥ مُلْكُ ٱلسَّمَٰوَٰتِ وَٱلْأَرْضِ وَٱللَّهُ عَلَىٰ كُلِّ شَىْءٍ شَهِيدٌ ۝٩ إِنَّ ٱلَّذِينَ فَتَنُوا۟ ٱلْمُؤْمِنِينَ وَٱلْمُؤْمِنَٰتِ ثُمَّ لَمْ يَتُوبُوا۟ فَلَهُمْ عَذَابُ جَهَنَّمَ وَلَهُمْ عَذَابُ ٱلْحَرِيقِ ۝١٠ إِنَّ ٱلَّذِينَ ءَامَنُوا۟ وَعَمِلُوا۟ ٱلصَّٰلِحَٰتِ لَهُمْ جَنَّٰتٌ تَجْرِى مِن تَحْتِهَا ٱلْأَنْهَٰرُ ذَٰلِكَ ٱلْفَوْزُ ٱلْكَبِيرُ ۝١١ إِنَّ بَطْشَ رَبِّكَ لَشَدِيدٌ ۝١٢ إِنَّهُۥ هُوَ يُبْدِئُ وَيُعِيدُ ۝١٣ وَهُوَ ٱلْغَفُورُ ٱلْوَدُودُ ۝١٤ ذُو ٱلْعَرْشِ ٱلْمَجِيدُ ۝١٥ فَعَّالٌ لِّمَا يُرِيدُ ۝١٦ هَلْ أَتَىٰكَ حَدِيثُ ٱلْجُنُودِ ۝١٧ فِرْعَوْنَ وَثَمُودَ ۝١٨ بَلِ ٱلَّذِينَ كَفَرُوا۟ فِى تَكْذِيبٍ ۝١٩ وَٱللَّهُ مِن وَرَآئِهِم مُّحِيطٌۢ ۝٢٠ بَلْ هُوَ قُرْءَانٌ مَّجِيدٌ ۝٢١ فِى لَوْحٍ مَّحْفُوظٍۭ ۝٢٢

٥٩٠

My Juz' 'Amma Journey

Write down as many examples as you can from the page:

Identify Makharij of 6 letters	Ghunnah	Madd	Elevated sounds

Noon Saakin & Tanween
Idgham: ------------------

Ikhfaa': ------------------

Iqlab: ------------------

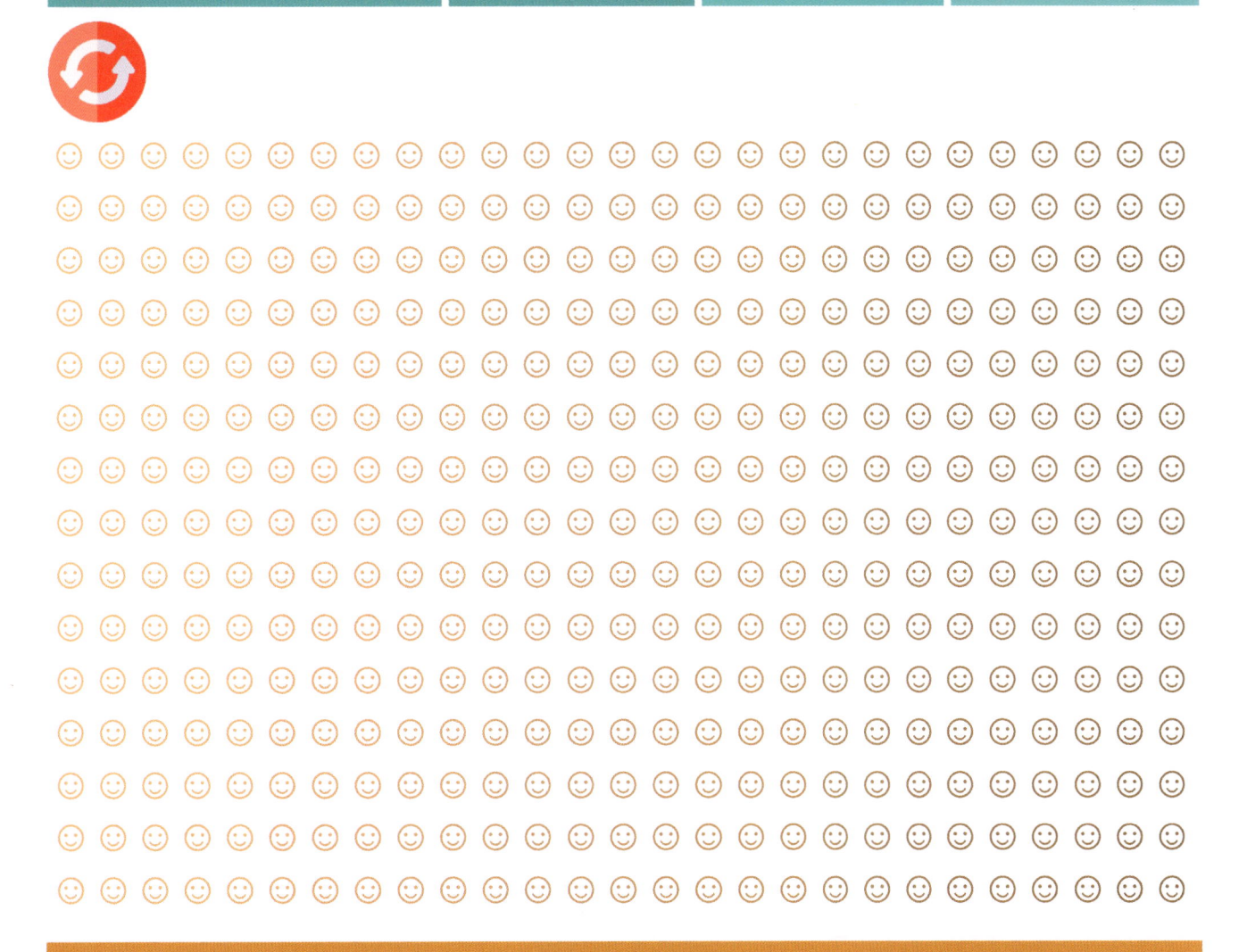

Meem Saakin
Idgham: ------------------

Ikhfaa': ------------------

Qalqalah

Hamzatul-wasl

40

My Juz' 'Amma Journey

Surah at-Tariq shows Allah's strong control and effective power.

	1-3. By the heaven, and by the night-comer. Do you know what the night-comer is? It is the star of piercing brightness.
	4. All human beings have angels over them, who guard them and write their deeds.
	5-9. So let man see from what he is created! He is created from a liquid gushing forth, proceeding from between the back-bone and the ribs. Verily, Allah is Able to bring him back to life on the Day when all the secrets will appear.
	10. Then, man will have no power, nor any helper.
	11, 12. By the sky which gives rain again and again. And by the earth which splits with the growth of trees and plants,
	13, 14. Verily! This Qur'an is the Word that separates the truth from falsehood; and it is not for amusement.
	15, 16. Those who deny what their messenger brought to them plan to reject his call. And I too plan to make the religion victorious and to disprove falsehood.
	17. So, O Messenger give the disbelievers a respite for a short while, and do not hasten their punishment and destruction.

Surah al-A'laa reminds us of Allah's favours, linking us to the Hereafter and releasing us from worldly obsessions.

	1-5. Glorify the Name of your Lord, the Most-High, Who has created everything and made it perfect, Who determined for all things their species, types and attributes and Who guided every creation to what is appropriate for it. And Who brings out the green grass for animals and then makes it dark stubble.
	6, 7. We shall make you O Messenger to recite the Qur'an, so you shall not forget it, except what Allah may will. He knows what is apparent and what is hidden.
	8. And We will make it easy for you O Messenger to do actions that please Us and enter you into Paradise.
	9, 10. Therefore, remind people in case the reminder benefits them. The one who fears Allah will pay heed to your reminder and benefit from it.

سُورَةُ الطَّارِقِ

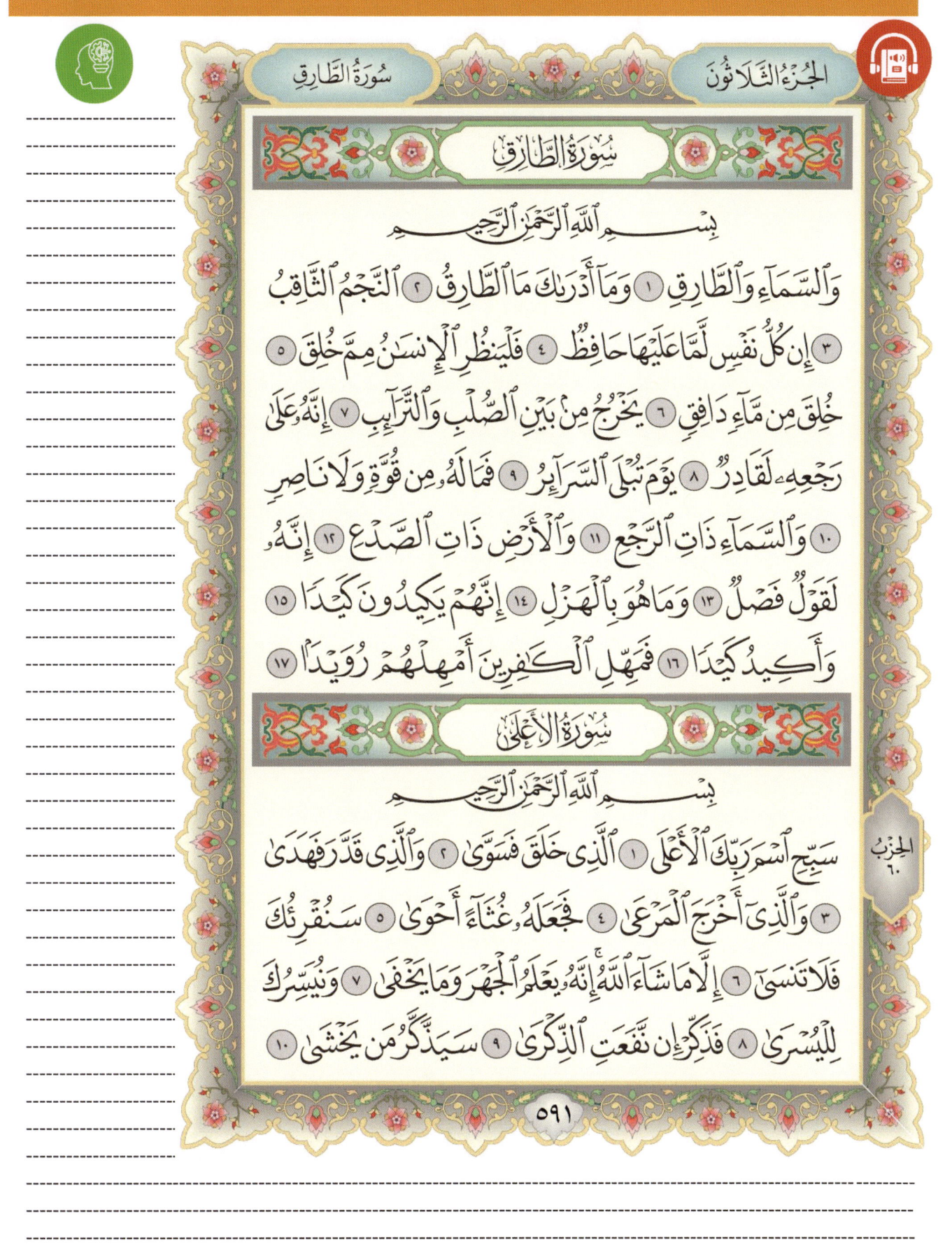

بِسْمِ اللَّهِ الرَّحْمَٰنِ الرَّحِيمِ

وَالسَّمَاءِ وَالطَّارِقِ ﴿١﴾ وَمَا أَدْرَاكَ مَا الطَّارِقُ ﴿٢﴾ النَّجْمُ الثَّاقِبُ ﴿٣﴾ إِن كُلُّ نَفْسٍ لَّمَّا عَلَيْهَا حَافِظٌ ﴿٤﴾ فَلْيَنظُرِ الْإِنسَانُ مِمَّ خُلِقَ ﴿٥﴾ خُلِقَ مِن مَّاءٍ دَافِقٍ ﴿٦﴾ يَخْرُجُ مِن بَيْنِ الصُّلْبِ وَالتَّرَائِبِ ﴿٧﴾ إِنَّهُ عَلَىٰ رَجْعِهِ لَقَادِرٌ ﴿٨﴾ يَوْمَ تُبْلَى السَّرَائِرُ ﴿٩﴾ فَمَا لَهُ مِن قُوَّةٍ وَلَا نَاصِرٍ ﴿١٠﴾ وَالسَّمَاءِ ذَاتِ الرَّجْعِ ﴿١١﴾ وَالْأَرْضِ ذَاتِ الصَّدْعِ ﴿١٢﴾ إِنَّهُ لَقَوْلٌ فَصْلٌ ﴿١٣﴾ وَمَا هُوَ بِالْهَزْلِ ﴿١٤﴾ إِنَّهُمْ يَكِيدُونَ كَيْدًا ﴿١٥﴾ وَأَكِيدُ كَيْدًا ﴿١٦﴾ فَمَهِّلِ الْكَافِرِينَ أَمْهِلْهُمْ رُوَيْدًا ﴿١٧﴾

سُورَةُ الْأَعْلَىٰ

بِسْمِ اللَّهِ الرَّحْمَٰنِ الرَّحِيمِ

سَبِّحِ اسْمَ رَبِّكَ الْأَعْلَى ﴿١﴾ الَّذِي خَلَقَ فَسَوَّىٰ ﴿٢﴾ وَالَّذِي قَدَّرَ فَهَدَىٰ ﴿٣﴾ وَالَّذِي أَخْرَجَ الْمَرْعَىٰ ﴿٤﴾ فَجَعَلَهُ غُثَاءً أَحْوَىٰ ﴿٥﴾ سَنُقْرِئُكَ فَلَا تَنسَىٰ ﴿٦﴾ إِلَّا مَا شَاءَ اللَّهُ ۚ إِنَّهُ يَعْلَمُ الْجَهْرَ وَمَا يَخْفَىٰ ﴿٧﴾ وَنُيَسِّرُكَ لِلْيُسْرَىٰ ﴿٨﴾ فَذَكِّرْ إِن نَّفَعَتِ الذِّكْرَىٰ ﴿٩﴾ سَيَذَّكَّرُ مَن يَخْشَىٰ ﴿١٠﴾

My Juz' 'Amma Journey

Write down as many examples as you can from the page:

Identify Makharij of 6 letters	Ghunnah	Madd	Elevated sounds
-------------------	-------------------	-------------------	-------------------
-------------------	-------------------	-------------------	-------------------
-------------------	-------------------	-------------------	-------------------
-------------------	-------------------	-------------------	-------------------
-------------------	-------------------	-------------------	-------------------
-------------------	-------------------	-------------------	-------------------

Noon Saakin & Tanween	Meem Saakin	Qalqalah	Hamzatul-wasl
Idgham: -------------------	Idgham: -------------	-------------------	-------------------
Ikhfaa': -------------------	Ikhfaa': -------------	-------------------	-------------------
Iqlab: -------------------		-------------------	-------------------

43

سورة الطارق

بِسْمِ اللَّهِ الرَّحْمَنِ الرَّحِيمِ

وَالسَّمَاءِ وَالطَّارِقِ ﴿١﴾ وَمَا أَدْرَاكَ مَا الطَّارِقُ ﴿٢﴾ النَّجْمُ الثَّاقِبُ ﴿٣﴾ إِن كُلُّ نَفْسٍ لَّمَّا عَلَيْهَا حَافِظٌ ﴿٤﴾ فَلْيَنظُرِ الْإِنسَانُ مِمَّ خُلِقَ ﴿٥﴾ خُلِقَ مِن مَّاءٍ دَافِقٍ ﴿٦﴾ يَخْرُجُ مِن بَيْنِ الصُّلْبِ وَالتَّرَائِبِ ﴿٧﴾ إِنَّهُ عَلَىٰ رَجْعِهِ لَقَادِرٌ ﴿٨﴾ يَوْمَ تُبْلَى السَّرَائِرُ ﴿٩﴾ فَمَا لَهُ مِن قُوَّةٍ وَلَا نَاصِرٍ ﴿١٠﴾ وَالسَّمَاءِ ذَاتِ الرَّجْعِ ﴿١١﴾ وَالْأَرْضِ ذَاتِ الصَّدْعِ ﴿١٢﴾ إِنَّهُ لَقَوْلٌ فَصْلٌ ﴿١٣﴾ وَمَا هُوَ بِالْهَزْلِ ﴿١٤﴾ إِنَّهُمْ يَكِيدُونَ كَيْدًا ﴿١٥﴾ وَأَكِيدُ كَيْدًا ﴿١٦﴾ فَمَهِّلِ الْكَافِرِينَ أَمْهِلْهُمْ رُوَيْدًا ﴿١٧﴾

سورة الأعلى

بِسْمِ اللَّهِ الرَّحْمَنِ الرَّحِيمِ

سَبِّحِ اسْمَ رَبِّكَ الْأَعْلَى ﴿١﴾ الَّذِي خَلَقَ فَسَوَّىٰ ﴿٢﴾ وَالَّذِي قَدَّرَ فَهَدَىٰ ﴿٣﴾ وَالَّذِي أَخْرَجَ الْمَرْعَىٰ ﴿٤﴾ فَجَعَلَهُ غُثَاءً أَحْوَىٰ ﴿٥﴾ سَنُقْرِئُكَ فَلَا تَنسَىٰ ﴿٦﴾ إِلَّا مَا شَاءَ اللَّهُ إِنَّهُ يَعْلَمُ الْجَهْرَ وَمَا يَخْفَىٰ ﴿٧﴾ وَنُيَسِّرُكَ لِلْيُسْرَىٰ ﴿٨﴾ فَذَكِّرْ إِن نَّفَعَتِ الذِّكْرَىٰ ﴿٩﴾ سَيَذَّكَّرُ مَن يَخْشَىٰ ﴿١٠﴾

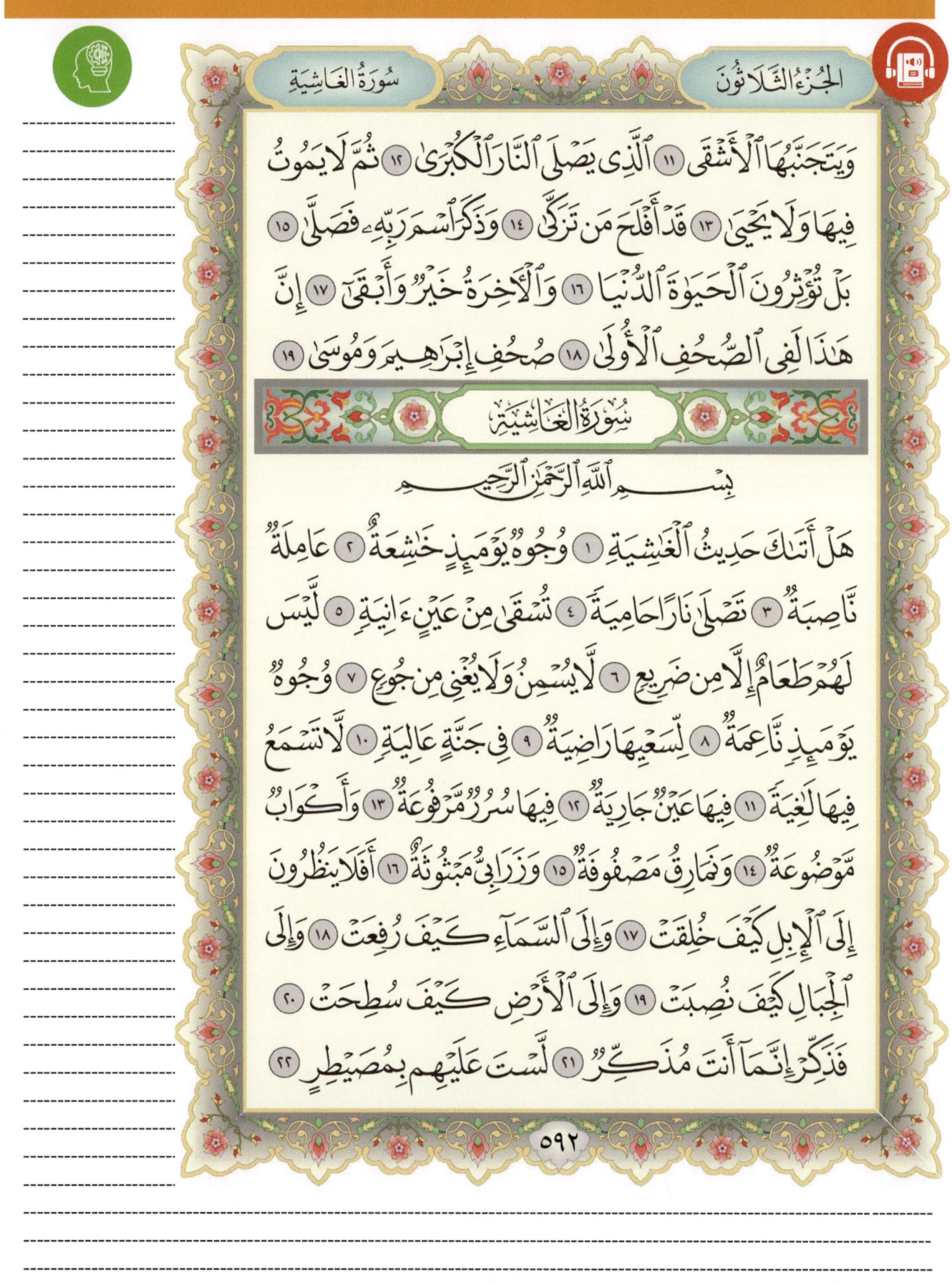

وَيَتَجَنَّبُهَا ٱلْأَشْقَى ۝ ٱلَّذِى يَصْلَى ٱلنَّارَ ٱلْكُبْرَىٰ ۝ ثُمَّ لَا يَمُوتُ فِيهَا وَلَا يَحْيَىٰ ۝ قَدْ أَفْلَحَ مَن تَزَكَّىٰ ۝ وَذَكَرَ ٱسْمَ رَبِّهِۦ فَصَلَّىٰ ۝ بَلْ تُؤْثِرُونَ ٱلْحَيَوٰةَ ٱلدُّنْيَا ۝ وَٱلْءَاخِرَةُ خَيْرٌ وَأَبْقَىٰٓ ۝ إِنَّ هَٰذَا لَفِى ٱلصُّحُفِ ٱلْأُولَىٰ ۝ صُحُفِ إِبْرَٰهِيمَ وَمُوسَىٰ ۝

سُورَةُ ٱلْغَاشِيَةِ

بِسْمِ ٱللَّهِ ٱلرَّحْمَٰنِ ٱلرَّحِيمِ

هَلْ أَتَىٰكَ حَدِيثُ ٱلْغَٰشِيَةِ ۝ وُجُوهٌ يَوْمَئِذٍ خَٰشِعَةٌ ۝ عَامِلَةٌ نَّاصِبَةٌ ۝ تَصْلَىٰ نَارًا حَامِيَةً ۝ تُسْقَىٰ مِنْ عَيْنٍ ءَانِيَةٍ ۝ لَّيْسَ لَهُمْ طَعَامٌ إِلَّا مِن ضَرِيعٍ ۝ لَّا يُسْمِنُ وَلَا يُغْنِى مِن جُوعٍ ۝ وُجُوهٌ يَوْمَئِذٍ نَّاعِمَةٌ ۝ لِّسَعْيِهَا رَاضِيَةٌ ۝ فِى جَنَّةٍ عَالِيَةٍ ۝ لَّا تَسْمَعُ فِيهَا لَٰغِيَةً ۝ فِيهَا عَيْنٌ جَارِيَةٌ ۝ فِيهَا سُرُرٌ مَّرْفُوعَةٌ ۝ وَأَكْوَابٌ مَّوْضُوعَةٌ ۝ وَنَمَارِقُ مَصْفُوفَةٌ ۝ وَزَرَابِىُّ مَبْثُوثَةٌ ۝ أَفَلَا يَنظُرُونَ إِلَى ٱلْإِبِلِ كَيْفَ خُلِقَتْ ۝ وَإِلَى ٱلسَّمَاءِ كَيْفَ رُفِعَتْ ۝ وَإِلَى ٱلْجِبَالِ كَيْفَ نُصِبَتْ ۝ وَإِلَى ٱلْأَرْضِ كَيْفَ سُطِحَتْ ۝ فَذَكِّرْ إِنَّمَا أَنتَ مُذَكِّرٌ ۝ لَّسْتَ عَلَيْهِم بِمُصَيْطِرٍ ۝

11-13. But the wretched will keep himself away from the reminder. He will enter the great Fire and taste its burning, wherein he will neither die to be in rest nor live a good living.

14, 15. Success will be achieved by him who purifies himself from idolatry and sins, remembers the Name of his Lord and establishes the prayers.

16, 17. Nay, you prefer the life of this world; although the Hereafter is better and more lasting.

18, 19. Verily! This advice is in the former Scriptures of Ibrahim and Musa.

Surah al-Ghashiyah reminds people about the Hereafter in respect of punishment and bliss. It also indicates signs of Allah's Power.

1. Has there come to you the news of the Day of Judgment that will overwhelm people with its horrors?

2, 3. Some faces, that Day, will be humiliated in the Hell fire, strained due to the chains that they will be dragged by and the shackles that they will be tied with.

4-7. They will enter in the hot blazing Fire. They will be given to drink from a boiling spring. Their only food will be a poisonous thorny plant, which will neither nourish them nor avail them against hunger.

8-15. Other faces, that Day, will be joyful, glad with their endeavour. They will be in a lofty Paradise, hearing neither harmful speech nor falsehood. Therein will be a running spring, thrones raised high, cups set at hand, cushions set in rows, and rich carpets spread out.

17. Do they not look at the camels, how they are created?

18. And at the heaven, how it is raised?

19. And at the mountains, how they are rooted?

20. And at the earth, how it is spread out?

21, 22. So remind them, O Messenger, you are only there to remind. You have not been given control over them.

الجزء الثلاثون — سورة الغاشية

وَيَتَجَنَّبُهَا ٱلْأَشْقَى ۞ ٱلَّذِى يَصْلَى ٱلنَّارَ ٱلْكُبْرَىٰ ۞ ثُمَّ لَا يَمُوتُ فِيهَا وَلَا يَحْيَىٰ ۞ قَدْ أَفْلَحَ مَن تَزَكَّىٰ ۞ وَذَكَرَ ٱسْمَ رَبِّهِ فَصَلَّىٰ ۞ بَلْ تُؤْثِرُونَ ٱلْحَيَوٰةَ ٱلدُّنْيَا ۞ وَٱلْآخِرَةُ خَيْرٌ وَأَبْقَىٰ ۞ إِنَّ هَٰذَا لَفِى ٱلصُّحُفِ ٱلْأُولَىٰ ۞ صُحُفِ إِبْرَٰهِيمَ وَمُوسَىٰ ۞

سورة الغاشية

بِسْمِ ٱللَّهِ ٱلرَّحْمَٰنِ ٱلرَّحِيمِ

هَلْ أَتَىٰكَ حَدِيثُ ٱلْغَاشِيَةِ ۞ وُجُوهٌ يَوْمَئِذٍ خَاشِعَةٌ ۞ عَامِلَةٌ نَّاصِبَةٌ ۞ تَصْلَىٰ نَارًا حَامِيَةً ۞ تُسْقَىٰ مِنْ عَيْنٍ ءَانِيَةٍ ۞ لَّيْسَ لَهُمْ طَعَامٌ إِلَّا مِن ضَرِيعٍ ۞ لَّا يُسْمِنُ وَلَا يُغْنِى مِن جُوعٍ ۞ وُجُوهٌ يَوْمَئِذٍ نَّاعِمَةٌ ۞ لِّسَعْيِهَا رَاضِيَةٌ ۞ فِى جَنَّةٍ عَالِيَةٍ ۞ لَّا تَسْمَعُ فِيهَا لَاغِيَةً ۞ فِيهَا عَيْنٌ جَارِيَةٌ ۞ فِيهَا سُرُرٌ مَّرْفُوعَةٌ ۞ وَأَكْوَابٌ مَّوْضُوعَةٌ ۞ وَنَمَارِقُ مَصْفُوفَةٌ ۞ وَزَرَابِىُّ مَبْثُوثَةٌ ۞ أَفَلَا يَنظُرُونَ إِلَى ٱلْإِبِلِ كَيْفَ خُلِقَتْ ۞ وَإِلَى ٱلسَّمَاءِ كَيْفَ رُفِعَتْ ۞ وَإِلَى ٱلْجِبَالِ كَيْفَ نُصِبَتْ ۞ وَإِلَى ٱلْأَرْضِ كَيْفَ سُطِحَتْ ۞ فَذَكِّرْ إِنَّمَا أَنتَ مُذَكِّرٌ ۞ لَّسْتَ عَلَيْهِم بِمُصَيْطِرٍ ۞

My Juz' 'Amma Journey

Write down as many examples as you can from the page:

Identify Makharij of 6 letters	Ghunnah	Madd	Elevated sounds

Noon Saakin & Tanween	Meem Saakin	Qalqalah	Hamzatul-wasl
Idgham: ——————————— Ikhfaa': ——————————— Iqlab: ———————————	Idgham: ——————————— Ikhfaa': ———————————		

My Juz' 'Amma Journey

23, 24. Except the one who turns away and disbelieves, for Allah will punish him with the greatest punishment.

25, 26. Verily, they will return to Us, and their reckoning will be for Us.

Surah al-Fajr presents Allah's Greatness and Power in the universe, the different conditions of humans, and the outcome of the deviants.

	1. By the dawn,		2. And by the ten nights of Dhul-Hijjah,
	3. And by the even and the odd of all the creations of Allah,		4. And by the night when it departs,

5. These oaths are sufficient proofs for men of understanding.

6-8. Did you, O Messenger, not think how your Lord dealt with 'Ad people, who were very tall like lofty pillars, the like of whom no one was created?

9. And with Thamud people, who cut out rocks in the valley to make dwellings?

10-14. And with Pharaoh, who had pegs to torture people on, who transgressed beyond bounds in the lands, and made therein much mischief? So, your Lord poured on them different kinds of severe torment. Verily, your Lord is Ever Watchful over them.

15. As for man, when his Lord tests him by giving him honour and gifts, then he says: "My Lord has honoured me."

16. But when He tests him by tightening his means of life, then he says: "My Lord has humiliated me!"

17. Nay! But you do not treat the orphans with kindness and generosity!

18. And do not encourage on the feeding of the needy!

19. And you greedily devour inheritance of the weak people,

20. And you love wealth with much love!

21, 22. Nay! When the earth is ground to powder, and when your Lord comes with the angels in rows,

الجزء الثلاثون — سورة الفجر

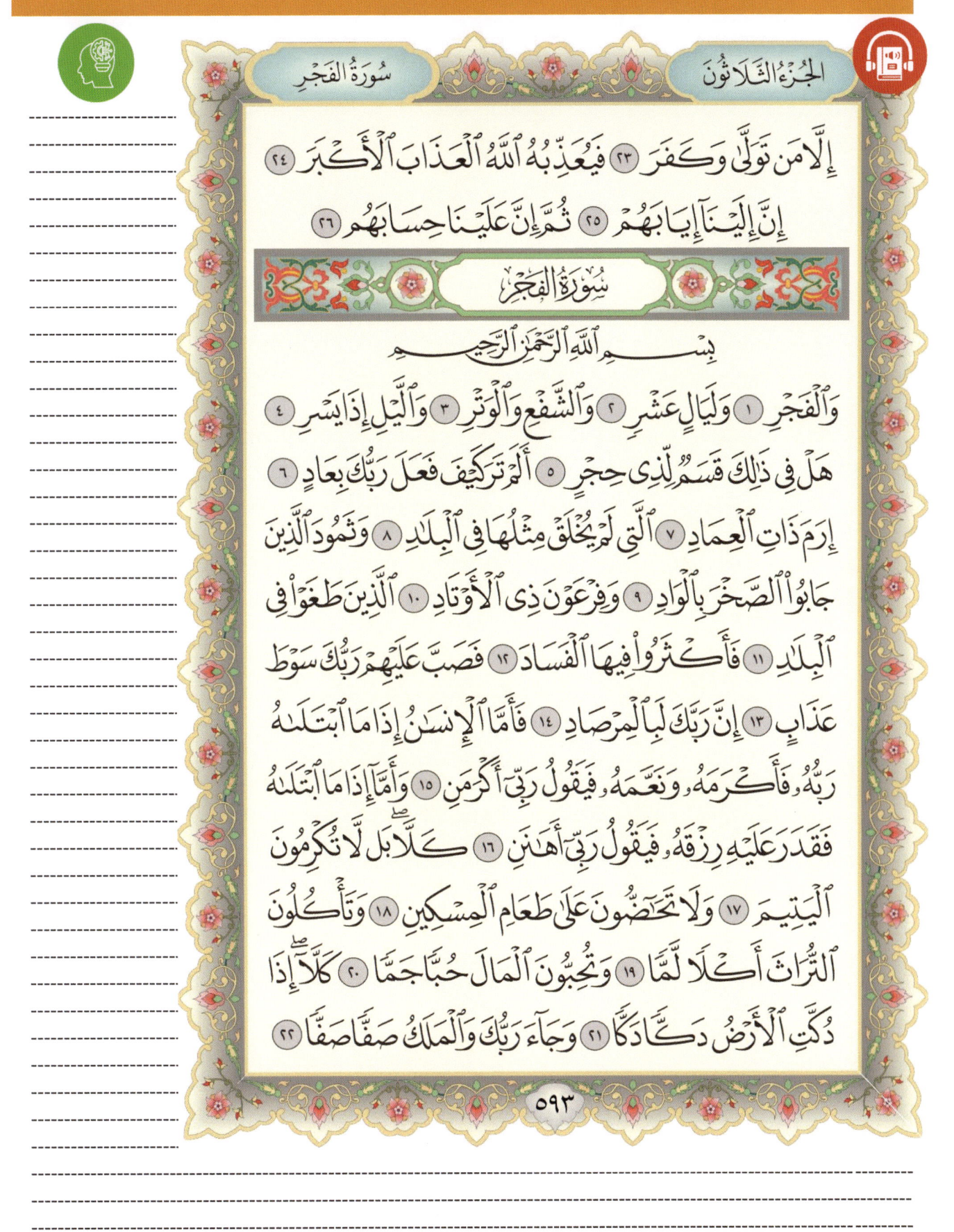

إِلَّا مَن تَوَلَّىٰ وَكَفَرَ ۝ فَيُعَذِّبُهُ ٱللَّهُ ٱلْعَذَابَ ٱلْأَكْبَرَ ۝ إِنَّ إِلَيْنَآ إِيَابَهُمْ ۝ ثُمَّ إِنَّ عَلَيْنَا حِسَابَهُم ۝

سُورَةُ الفَجْرِ

بِسْمِ ٱللَّهِ ٱلرَّحْمَٰنِ ٱلرَّحِيمِ

وَٱلْفَجْرِ ۝ وَلَيَالٍ عَشْرٍ ۝ وَٱلشَّفْعِ وَٱلْوَتْرِ ۝ وَٱلَّيْلِ إِذَا يَسْرِ ۝ هَلْ فِي ذَٰلِكَ قَسَمٌ لِّذِي حِجْرٍ ۝ أَلَمْ تَرَ كَيْفَ فَعَلَ رَبُّكَ بِعَادٍ ۝ إِرَمَ ذَاتِ ٱلْعِمَادِ ۝ ٱلَّتِي لَمْ يُخْلَقْ مِثْلُهَا فِي ٱلْبِلَادِ ۝ وَثَمُودَ ٱلَّذِينَ جَابُوا۟ ٱلصَّخْرَ بِٱلْوَادِ ۝ وَفِرْعَوْنَ ذِي ٱلْأَوْتَادِ ۝ ٱلَّذِينَ طَغَوْا۟ فِي ٱلْبِلَادِ ۝ فَأَكْثَرُوا۟ فِيهَا ٱلْفَسَادَ ۝ فَصَبَّ عَلَيْهِمْ رَبُّكَ سَوْطَ عَذَابٍ ۝ إِنَّ رَبَّكَ لَبِٱلْمِرْصَادِ ۝ فَأَمَّا ٱلْإِنسَٰنُ إِذَا مَا ٱبْتَلَىٰهُ رَبُّهُۥ فَأَكْرَمَهُۥ وَنَعَّمَهُۥ فَيَقُولُ رَبِّي أَكْرَمَنِ ۝ وَأَمَّآ إِذَا مَا ٱبْتَلَىٰهُ فَقَدَرَ عَلَيْهِ رِزْقَهُۥ فَيَقُولُ رَبِّي أَهَٰنَنِ ۝ كَلَّا ۖ بَل لَّا تُكْرِمُونَ ٱلْيَتِيمَ ۝ وَلَا تَحَٰٓضُّونَ عَلَىٰ طَعَامِ ٱلْمِسْكِينِ ۝ وَتَأْكُلُونَ ٱلتُّرَاثَ أَكْلًا لَّمًّا ۝ وَتُحِبُّونَ ٱلْمَالَ حُبًّا جَمًّا ۝ كَلَّآ إِذَا دُكَّتِ ٱلْأَرْضُ دَكًّا دَكًّا ۝ وَجَآءَ رَبُّكَ وَٱلْمَلَكُ صَفًّا صَفًّا ۝

٥٩٣

My Juz' 'Amma Journey

Write down as many examples as you can from the page:

Identify Makharij of 6 letters	Ghunnah	Madd	Elevated sounds

Noon Saakin & Tanween	Meem Saakin	Qalqalah	Hamzatul-wasl
Idgham: _____ Ikhfaa': _____ Iqlab: _____	Idgham: _____ Ikhfaa': _____		

51

الجزء الثلاثون ۞ سورة الفجر

إِلَّا مَن تَوَلَّىٰ وَكَفَرَ ۝ فَيُعَذِّبُهُ ٱللَّهُ ٱلۡعَذَابَ ٱلۡأَكۡبَرَ ۝ إِنَّ إِلَيۡنَآ إِيَابَهُمۡ ۝ ثُمَّ إِنَّ عَلَيۡنَا حِسَابَهُم ۝

سُورَةُ الفَجْرِ

بِسْمِ اللَّهِ الرَّحْمَٰنِ الرَّحِيمِ

وَٱلۡفَجۡرِ ۝ وَلَيَالٍ عَشۡرٍ ۝ وَٱلشَّفۡعِ وَٱلۡوَتۡرِ ۝ وَٱلَّيۡلِ إِذَا يَسۡرِ ۝ هَلۡ فِي ذَٰلِكَ قَسَمٌ لِّذِي حِجۡرٍ ۝ أَلَمۡ تَرَ كَيۡفَ فَعَلَ رَبُّكَ بِعَادٍ ۝ إِرَمَ ذَاتِ ٱلۡعِمَادِ ۝ ٱلَّتِي لَمۡ يُخۡلَقۡ مِثۡلُهَا فِي ٱلۡبِلَٰدِ ۝ وَثَمُودَ ٱلَّذِينَ جَابُوا۟ ٱلصَّخۡرَ بِٱلۡوَادِ ۝ وَفِرۡعَوۡنَ ذِي ٱلۡأَوۡتَادِ ۝ ٱلَّذِينَ طَغَوۡا۟ فِي ٱلۡبِلَٰدِ ۝ فَأَكۡثَرُوا۟ فِيهَا ٱلۡفَسَادَ ۝ فَصَبَّ عَلَيۡهِمۡ رَبُّكَ سَوۡطَ عَذَابٍ ۝ إِنَّ رَبَّكَ لَبِٱلۡمِرۡصَادِ ۝ فَأَمَّا ٱلۡإِنسَٰنُ إِذَا مَا ٱبۡتَلَىٰهُ رَبُّهُۥ فَأَكۡرَمَهُۥ وَنَعَّمَهُۥ فَيَقُولُ رَبِّيٓ أَكۡرَمَنِ ۝ وَأَمَّآ إِذَا مَا ٱبۡتَلَىٰهُ فَقَدَرَ عَلَيۡهِ رِزۡقَهُۥ فَيَقُولُ رَبِّيٓ أَهَٰنَنِ ۝ كَلَّا ۖ بَل لَّا تُكۡرِمُونَ ٱلۡيَتِيمَ ۝ وَلَا تَحَٰٓضُّونَ عَلَىٰ طَعَامِ ٱلۡمِسۡكِينِ ۝ وَتَأۡكُلُونَ ٱلتُّرَاثَ أَكۡلًا لَّمًّا ۝ وَتُحِبُّونَ ٱلۡمَالَ حُبًّا جَمًّا ۝ كَلَّآ إِذَا دُكَّتِ ٱلۡأَرۡضُ دَكًّا دَكًّا ۝ وَجَآءَ رَبُّكَ وَٱلۡمَلَكُ صَفًّا صَفًّا ۝

٥٩٣

الجزء الثلاثون — سورة البلد

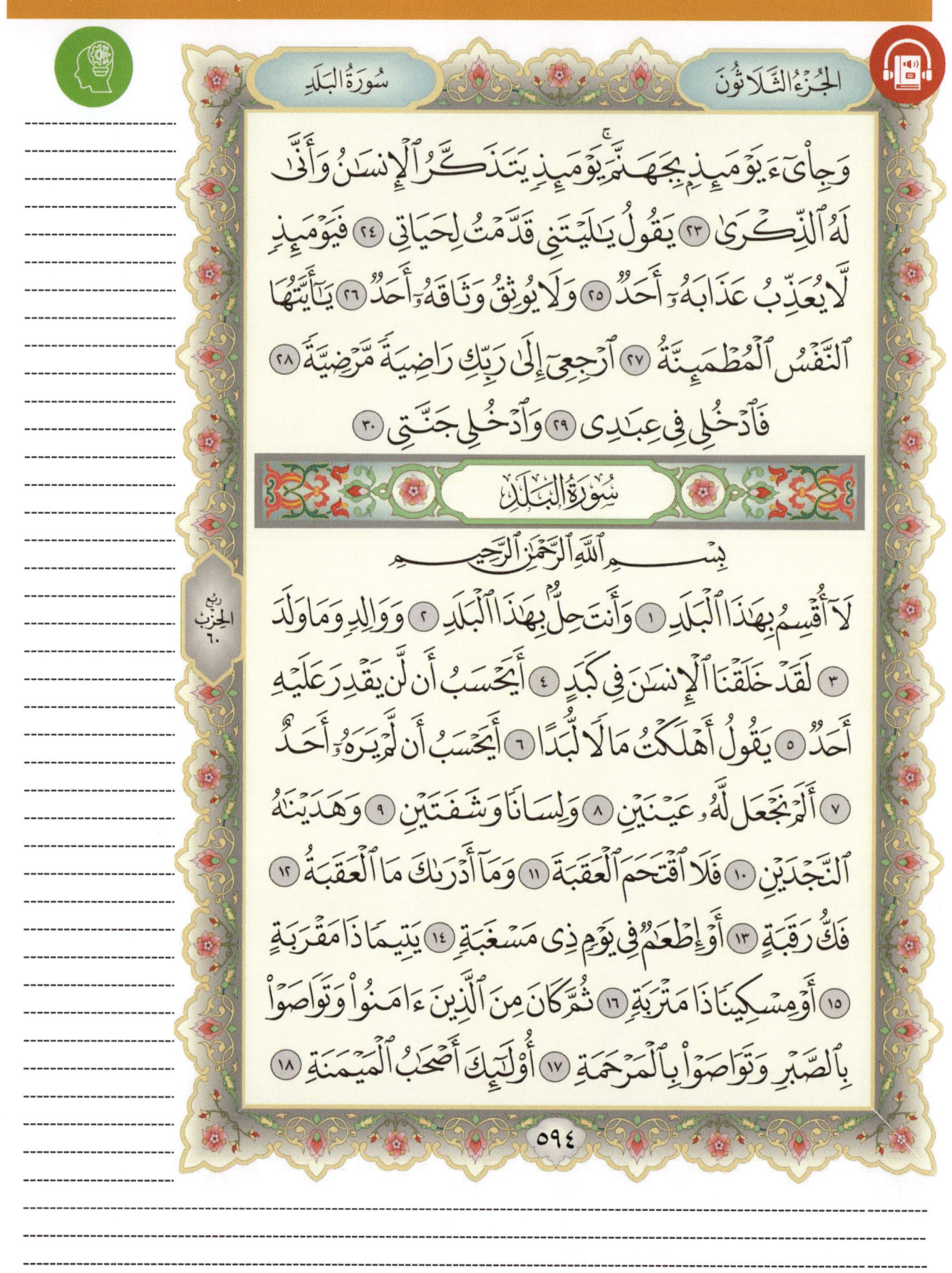

وَجِايٓءَ يَوْمَئِذٍۭ بِجَهَنَّمَ ۚ يَوْمَئِذٍ يَتَذَكَّرُ ٱلْإِنسَٰنُ وَأَنَّىٰ لَهُ ٱلذِّكْرَىٰ ۝٢٣ يَقُولُ يَٰلَيْتَنِى قَدَّمْتُ لِحَيَاتِى ۝٢٤ فَيَوْمَئِذٍ لَّا يُعَذِّبُ عَذَابَهُۥٓ أَحَدٌ ۝٢٥ وَلَا يُوثِقُ وَثَاقَهُۥٓ أَحَدٌ ۝٢٦ يَٰٓأَيَّتُهَا ٱلنَّفْسُ ٱلْمُطْمَئِنَّةُ ۝٢٧ ٱرْجِعِىٓ إِلَىٰ رَبِّكِ رَاضِيَةً مَّرْضِيَّةً ۝٢٨ فَٱدْخُلِى فِى عِبَٰدِى ۝٢٩ وَٱدْخُلِى جَنَّتِى ۝٣٠

سُورَةُ البَلَدِ

بِسْمِ ٱللَّهِ ٱلرَّحْمَٰنِ ٱلرَّحِيمِ

لَآ أُقْسِمُ بِهَٰذَا ٱلْبَلَدِ ۝١ وَأَنتَ حِلٌّۢ بِهَٰذَا ٱلْبَلَدِ ۝٢ وَوَالِدٍ وَمَا وَلَدَ ۝٣ لَقَدْ خَلَقْنَا ٱلْإِنسَٰنَ فِى كَبَدٍ ۝٤ أَيَحْسَبُ أَن لَّن يَقْدِرَ عَلَيْهِ أَحَدٌ ۝٥ يَقُولُ أَهْلَكْتُ مَالًا لُّبَدًا ۝٦ أَيَحْسَبُ أَن لَّمْ يَرَهُۥٓ أَحَدٌ ۝٧ أَلَمْ نَجْعَل لَّهُۥ عَيْنَيْنِ ۝٨ وَلِسَانًا وَشَفَتَيْنِ ۝٩ وَهَدَيْنَٰهُ ٱلنَّجْدَيْنِ ۝١٠ فَلَا ٱقْتَحَمَ ٱلْعَقَبَةَ ۝١١ وَمَآ أَدْرَىٰكَ مَا ٱلْعَقَبَةُ ۝١٢ فَكُّ رَقَبَةٍ ۝١٣ أَوْ إِطْعَٰمٌ فِى يَوْمٍ ذِى مَسْغَبَةٍ ۝١٤ يَتِيمًا ذَا مَقْرَبَةٍ ۝١٥ أَوْ مِسْكِينًا ذَا مَتْرَبَةٍ ۝١٦ ثُمَّ كَانَ مِنَ ٱلَّذِينَ ءَامَنُوا۟ وَتَوَاصَوْا۟ بِٱلصَّبْرِ وَتَوَاصَوْا۟ بِٱلْمَرْحَمَةِ ۝١٧ أُو۟لَٰٓئِكَ أَصْحَٰبُ ٱلْمَيْمَنَةِ ۝١٨

٥٩٤

23, 24. And when Hell will be brought near that Day, then man will remember; but how will this benefit? He will say: "I wish I had sent forth good deeds for this life!"

25, 26. So, on that Day, none will punish as Allah will punish. And none will bind the disbelievers as Allah will bind.

27-30. It will be said to the pious: "O assured soul! Come back to your Lord, Well-pleased and well-pleasing! Enter among My honoured slaves and enter My Paradise!"

Surah al-Balad focuses on the human, between the effect of disbelief and ascending in mercy and faith.

1. I swear by the city of Makkah.

2. And you, O Messenger, were allowed to fight the disbelievers on the Day of the Conquest of Makkah in that city.

3. And I swear by Adam, the begetter, and by his progeny, that which he begot;

4. Verily, We have created man in fatigue.

5-7. He thinks that none can overcome him and says boastfully: "I have wasted wealth in abundance!" He thinks that none sees him!

8, 9. Have We not made for him a pair of eyes, a tongue and a pair of lips?

10. And shown him the two ways of good and evil?

11-17. But he has made no effort to cross the steep path. Do you know what the steep path is? It is freeing a slave or giving food in a day of hunger to a relative orphan or to a needy afflicted with misery. And before all this, becoming one of those who believe and recommend one another to patience and compassion.

18. They are those on the right-hand side, the dwellers of Paradise.

سورة البلد — الجزء الثلاثون

وَجِا۟ىَٓ يَوْمَئِذٍۭ بِجَهَنَّمَ ۚ يَوْمَئِذٍ يَتَذَكَّرُ ٱلْإِنسَٰنُ وَأَنَّىٰ لَهُ ٱلذِّكْرَىٰ ۝ يَقُولُ يَٰلَيْتَنِى قَدَّمْتُ لِحَيَاتِى ۝ فَيَوْمَئِذٍ لَّا يُعَذِّبُ عَذَابَهُۥٓ أَحَدٌ ۝ وَلَا يُوثِقُ وَثَاقَهُۥٓ أَحَدٌ ۝ يَٰٓأَيَّتُهَا ٱلنَّفْسُ ٱلْمُطْمَئِنَّةُ ۝ ٱرْجِعِىٓ إِلَىٰ رَبِّكِ رَاضِيَةً مَّرْضِيَّةً ۝ فَٱدْخُلِى فِى عِبَٰدِى ۝ وَٱدْخُلِى جَنَّتِى ۝

سورة البلد

بِسْمِ ٱللَّهِ ٱلرَّحْمَٰنِ ٱلرَّحِيمِ

لَآ أُقْسِمُ بِهَٰذَا ٱلْبَلَدِ ۝ وَأَنتَ حِلٌّۢ بِهَٰذَا ٱلْبَلَدِ ۝ وَوَالِدٍ وَمَا وَلَدَ ۝ لَقَدْ خَلَقْنَا ٱلْإِنسَٰنَ فِى كَبَدٍ ۝ أَيَحْسَبُ أَن لَّن يَقْدِرَ عَلَيْهِ أَحَدٌ ۝ يَقُولُ أَهْلَكْتُ مَالًا لُّبَدًا ۝ أَيَحْسَبُ أَن لَّمْ يَرَهُۥٓ أَحَدٌ ۝ أَلَمْ نَجْعَل لَّهُۥ عَيْنَيْنِ ۝ وَلِسَانًا وَشَفَتَيْنِ ۝ وَهَدَيْنَٰهُ ٱلنَّجْدَيْنِ ۝ فَلَا ٱقْتَحَمَ ٱلْعَقَبَةَ ۝ وَمَآ أَدْرَىٰكَ مَا ٱلْعَقَبَةُ ۝ فَكُّ رَقَبَةٍ ۝ أَوْ إِطْعَٰمٌ فِى يَوْمٍ ذِى مَسْغَبَةٍ ۝ يَتِيمًا ذَا مَقْرَبَةٍ ۝ أَوْ مِسْكِينًا ذَا مَتْرَبَةٍ ۝ ثُمَّ كَانَ مِنَ ٱلَّذِينَ ءَامَنُوا۟ وَتَوَاصَوْا۟ بِٱلصَّبْرِ وَتَوَاصَوْا۟ بِٱلْمَرْحَمَةِ ۝ أُو۟لَٰٓئِكَ أَصْحَٰبُ ٱلْمَيْمَنَةِ ۝

٥٩٤

My Juz' 'Amma Journey

Write down as many examples as you can from the page:

Identify Makharij of 6 letters	Ghunnah	Madd	Elevated sounds

Noon Saakin & Tanween	Meem Saakin	Qalqalah	Hamzatul-wasl
Idgham:	Idgham:		
Ikhfaa':	Ikhfaa':		
Iqlab:			

My Juz' 'Amma Journey

19, 20. But those who disbelieved in Our verses, they are those on the left-hand side, the Fire will be shut over them.

Surah ash-Shams shows Allah's signs and blessings on Earth. It also speaks about people and their conditions, in order to purify their souls and warn them from disobedience.

1, 2. By the sun and its brightness. And by the moon as it follows it.

3, 4. By the day as it shows up the sun's brightness. And by the night as it conceals the sun.

5, 6. By the heaven and Him Who built it. And by the earth and Him Who spread it.

7-10. By the soul and Him Who perfected it in proportion and showed it what is wrong and what is right. He who purifies himself will be successful, and he who corrupts himself will be a loser.

11-15. Thamud people denied their Prophet and transgressed. The most wicked man among them went to kill the she-camel, but Salih, Allah's Messenger, said to them: "Be cautious! Fear the evil end. This is the she-camel of Allah! Do not harm or bar it from having its drink!" However, they denied him and killed it. So, their Lord destroyed them, fearing no reproach over His actions.

Surah al-Lail focuses on the souls and their deeds, to make the difference clear between the believers and the disbelievers.

1, 2. By the night as it envelops the world, and by the day as it appears in brightness.

3. And by Him Who created male and female.

4. Certainly, your efforts and deeds are different in aims and purposes.

5, 6. As for him who gives in charity, keeps his duty to Allah, fears Him and believes in goodness;

7. We will make smooth for him the path of goodness.

8, 9. But he who is a greedy miser, thinks himself self-sufficient and disbelieves in the goodness;

57

الجزء الثلاثون — سُورَةُ الشَّمْسِ

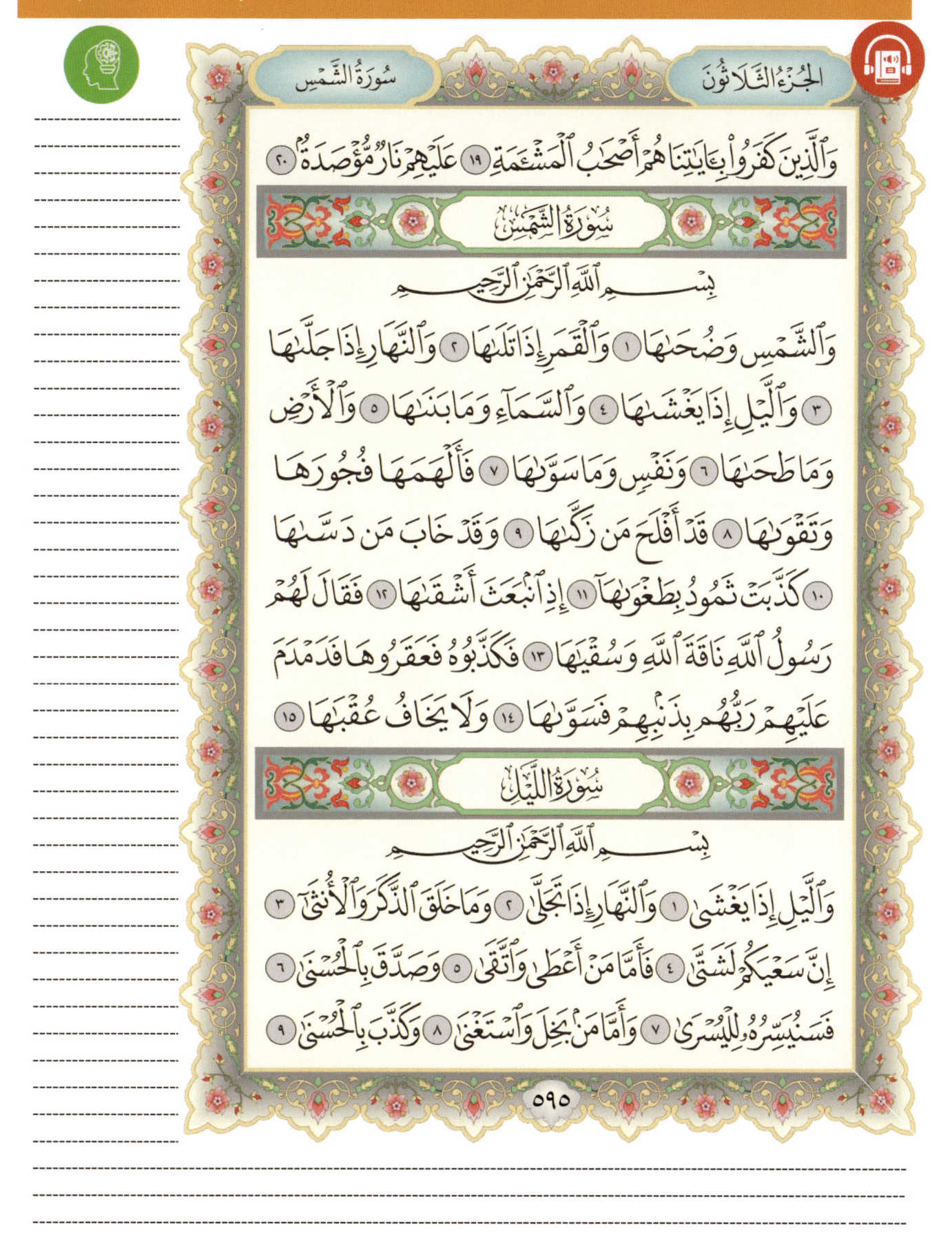

وَالَّذِينَ كَفَرُوا بِآيَاتِنَا هُمْ أَصْحَابُ الْمَشْأَمَةِ ۝١٩ عَلَيْهِمْ نَارٌ مُّؤْصَدَةٌ ۝٢٠

سُورَةُ الشَّمْسِ

بِسْمِ اللَّهِ الرَّحْمَٰنِ الرَّحِيمِ

وَالشَّمْسِ وَضُحَاهَا ۝١ وَالْقَمَرِ إِذَا تَلَاهَا ۝٢ وَالنَّهَارِ إِذَا جَلَّاهَا ۝٣ وَاللَّيْلِ إِذَا يَغْشَاهَا ۝٤ وَالسَّمَاءِ وَمَا بَنَاهَا ۝٥ وَالْأَرْضِ وَمَا طَحَاهَا ۝٦ وَنَفْسٍ وَمَا سَوَّاهَا ۝٧ فَأَلْهَمَهَا فُجُورَهَا وَتَقْوَاهَا ۝٨ قَدْ أَفْلَحَ مَن زَكَّاهَا ۝٩ وَقَدْ خَابَ مَن دَسَّاهَا ۝١٠ كَذَّبَتْ ثَمُودُ بِطَغْوَاهَا ۝١١ إِذِ انبَعَثَ أَشْقَاهَا ۝١٢ فَقَالَ لَهُمْ رَسُولُ اللَّهِ نَاقَةَ اللَّهِ وَسُقْيَاهَا ۝١٣ فَكَذَّبُوهُ فَعَقَرُوهَا فَدَمْدَمَ عَلَيْهِمْ رَبُّهُم بِذَنبِهِمْ فَسَوَّاهَا ۝١٤ وَلَا يَخَافُ عُقْبَاهَا ۝١٥

سُورَةُ اللَّيْلِ

بِسْمِ اللَّهِ الرَّحْمَٰنِ الرَّحِيمِ

وَاللَّيْلِ إِذَا يَغْشَىٰ ۝١ وَالنَّهَارِ إِذَا تَجَلَّىٰ ۝٢ وَمَا خَلَقَ الذَّكَرَ وَالْأُنثَىٰ ۝٣ إِنَّ سَعْيَكُمْ لَشَتَّىٰ ۝٤ فَأَمَّا مَنْ أَعْطَىٰ وَاتَّقَىٰ ۝٥ وَصَدَّقَ بِالْحُسْنَىٰ ۝٦ فَسَنُيَسِّرُهُ لِلْيُسْرَىٰ ۝٧ وَأَمَّا مَن بَخِلَ وَاسْتَغْنَىٰ ۝٨ وَكَذَّبَ بِالْحُسْنَىٰ ۝٩

٥٩٥

My Juz' 'Amma Journey

Write down as many examples as you can from the page:

Identify Makharij of 6 letters	Ghunnah	Madd	Elevated sounds

Noon Saakin & Tanween
Idgham: ------------------
Ikhfaa': ------------------
Iqlab: ------------------

Meem Saakin
Idgham: ------------------
Ikhfaa': ------------------

Qalqalah

Hamzatul-wasl

الجزء الثلاثون ۞ سورة الشمس

وَٱلَّذِينَ كَفَرُوا۟ بِـَٔايَـٰتِنَا هُمْ أَصْحَـٰبُ ٱلْمَشْـَٔمَةِ ۩ عَلَيْهِمْ نَارٌ مُّؤْصَدَةٌۢ ۩

سُورَةُ ٱلشَّمْسِ

بِسْمِ ٱللَّهِ ٱلرَّحْمَـٰنِ ٱلرَّحِيمِ

وَٱلشَّمْسِ وَضُحَىٰهَا ۩ وَٱلْقَمَرِ إِذَا تَلَىٰهَا ۩ وَٱلنَّهَارِ إِذَا جَلَّىٰهَا ۩ وَٱلَّيْلِ إِذَا يَغْشَىٰهَا ۩ وَٱلسَّمَآءِ وَمَا بَنَىٰهَا ۩ وَٱلْأَرْضِ وَمَا طَحَىٰهَا ۩ وَنَفْسٍ وَمَا سَوَّىٰهَا ۩ فَأَلْهَمَهَا فُجُورَهَا وَتَقْوَىٰهَا ۩ قَدْ أَفْلَحَ مَن زَكَّىٰهَا ۩ وَقَدْ خَابَ مَن دَسَّىٰهَا ۩ كَذَّبَتْ ثَمُودُ بِطَغْوَىٰهَآ ۩ إِذِ ٱنۢبَعَثَ أَشْقَىٰهَا ۩ فَقَالَ لَهُمْ رَسُولُ ٱللَّهِ نَاقَةَ ٱللَّهِ وَسُقْيَـٰهَا ۩ فَكَذَّبُوهُ فَعَقَرُوهَا فَدَمْدَمَ عَلَيْهِمْ رَبُّهُم بِذَنۢبِهِمْ فَسَوَّىٰهَا ۩ وَلَا يَخَافُ عُقْبَـٰهَا ۩

سُورَةُ ٱلَّيْلِ

بِسْمِ ٱللَّهِ ٱلرَّحْمَـٰنِ ٱلرَّحِيمِ

وَٱلَّيْلِ إِذَا يَغْشَىٰ ۩ وَٱلنَّهَارِ إِذَا تَجَلَّىٰ ۩ وَمَا خَلَقَ ٱلذَّكَرَ وَٱلْأُنثَىٰٓ ۩ إِنَّ سَعْيَكُمْ لَشَتَّىٰ ۩ فَأَمَّا مَنْ أَعْطَىٰ وَٱتَّقَىٰ ۩ وَصَدَّقَ بِٱلْحُسْنَىٰ ۩ فَسَنُيَسِّرُهُۥ لِلْيُسْرَىٰ ۩ وَأَمَّا مَنۢ بَخِلَ وَٱسْتَغْنَىٰ ۩ وَكَذَّبَ بِٱلْحُسْنَىٰ ۩

٥٩٥

سُورَةُ الضُّحَى – الجزء الثلاثون

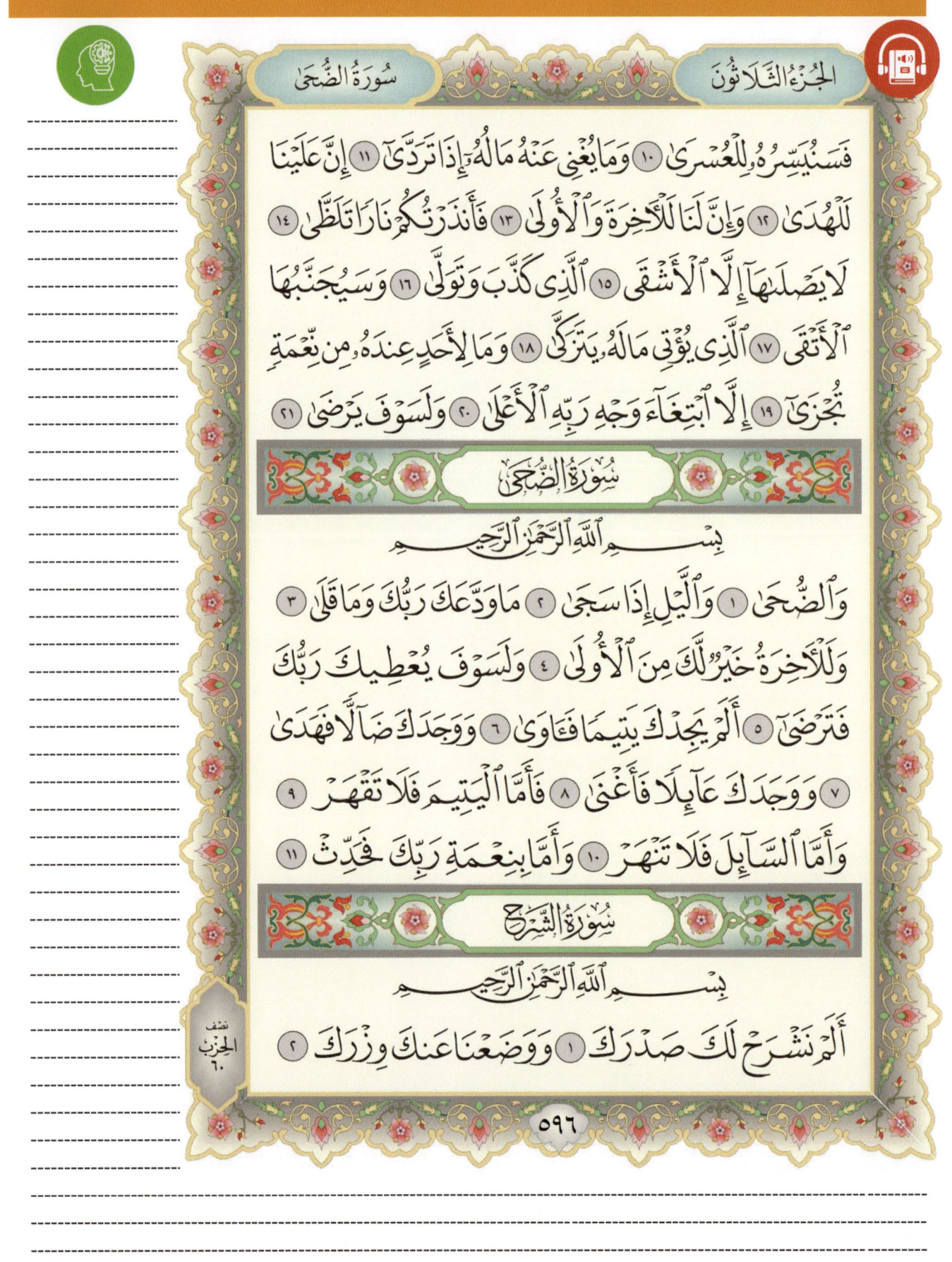

فَسَنُيَسِّرُهُ لِلْعُسْرَىٰ ۝ وَمَا يُغْنِي عَنْهُ مَالُهُ إِذَا تَرَدَّىٰ ۝ إِنَّ عَلَيْنَا لَلْهُدَىٰ ۝ وَإِنَّ لَنَا لَلْآخِرَةَ وَالْأُولَىٰ ۝ فَأَنذَرْتُكُمْ نَارًا تَلَظَّىٰ ۝ لَا يَصْلَاهَا إِلَّا الْأَشْقَى ۝ الَّذِي كَذَّبَ وَتَوَلَّىٰ ۝ وَسَيُجَنَّبُهَا الْأَتْقَى ۝ الَّذِي يُؤْتِي مَالَهُ يَتَزَكَّىٰ ۝ وَمَا لِأَحَدٍ عِندَهُ مِن نِّعْمَةٍ تُجْزَىٰ ۝ إِلَّا ابْتِغَاءَ وَجْهِ رَبِّهِ الْأَعْلَىٰ ۝ وَلَسَوْفَ يَرْضَىٰ ۝

سُورَةُ الضُّحَى

بِسْمِ اللَّهِ الرَّحْمَٰنِ الرَّحِيمِ

وَالضُّحَىٰ ۝ وَاللَّيْلِ إِذَا سَجَىٰ ۝ مَا وَدَّعَكَ رَبُّكَ وَمَا قَلَىٰ ۝ وَلَلْآخِرَةُ خَيْرٌ لَّكَ مِنَ الْأُولَىٰ ۝ وَلَسَوْفَ يُعْطِيكَ رَبُّكَ فَتَرْضَىٰ ۝ أَلَمْ يَجِدْكَ يَتِيمًا فَآوَىٰ ۝ وَوَجَدَكَ ضَالًّا فَهَدَىٰ ۝ وَوَجَدَكَ عَائِلًا فَأَغْنَىٰ ۝ فَأَمَّا الْيَتِيمَ فَلَا تَقْهَرْ ۝ وَأَمَّا السَّائِلَ فَلَا تَنْهَرْ ۝ وَأَمَّا بِنِعْمَةِ رَبِّكَ فَحَدِّثْ ۝

سُورَةُ الشَّرْحِ

بِسْمِ اللَّهِ الرَّحْمَٰنِ الرَّحِيمِ

أَلَمْ نَشْرَحْ لَكَ صَدْرَكَ ۝ وَوَضَعْنَا عَنكَ وِزْرَكَ ۝

نصف الحزب ٦٠

٥٩٦

My Juz' 'Amma Journey

10. We will make easy for him the path of evil.

11. His wealth, that he is miserly with, will not benefit him at all when he dies and enters Hell.

12, 13. Truly! Ours it is to give guidance, and truly, unto Us belong the Hereafter and this world.

14-16. Therefore, I have warned you of a Fire blazing fiercely; none shall enter it except the most wretched, who denies and turns away.

17-21. And the righteous will be far removed from Hell, who spends his wealth to increase in self-purification, and expects no reward from anyone in return, except for the Face of his Lord, the Most High. He surely will be pleased in Paradise.

Surah ad-Duha shows the favours Allah gave to His Prophet ﷺ, to put him at ease as well as reminding the believers to be grateful.

1, 2. By the forenoon; and by the night when it darkens.

3, 4. Your Lord, O Messenger, has neither deserted you nor hated you. And indeed, the Hereafter is better for you than the present life of this world.

5. And verily, your Lord will give you all good so that you shall be well-pleased.

6. Did He not find you, O Messenger, an orphan and gave you a refuge?

7. And He found you unaware of the Qur'an and guided you?

8. And He found you poor, and made you self-sufficient?

9-11. Therefore, do not treat the orphan with oppression and do not repulse the beggar; and speak about the Grace of your Lord.

Surah ash-Sharh highlights the completion of Allah's favours upon His Prophet ﷺ and what this requires

1. Have We not opened your chest, O Messenger ﷺ, for accepting the truth?

2, 3. And removed from you your burden which weighed down your back (by helping you in your da'wa and making your mission clear)?

الجزء الثلاثون سُورَةُ الضُّحَى

فَسَنُيَسِّرُهُۥ لِلْعُسْرَىٰ ۝ وَمَا يُغْنِى عَنْهُ مَالُهُۥٓ إِذَا تَرَدَّىٰٓ ۝ إِنَّ عَلَيْنَا لَلْهُدَىٰ ۝ وَإِنَّ لَنَا لَلْءَاخِرَةَ وَٱلْأُولَىٰ ۝ فَأَنذَرْتُكُمْ نَارًا تَلَظَّىٰ ۝ لَا يَصْلَىٰهَآ إِلَّا ٱلْأَشْقَى ۝ ٱلَّذِى كَذَّبَ وَتَوَلَّىٰ ۝ وَسَيُجَنَّبُهَا ٱلْأَتْقَى ۝ ٱلَّذِى يُؤْتِى مَالَهُۥ يَتَزَكَّىٰ ۝ وَمَا لِأَحَدٍ عِندَهُۥ مِن نِّعْمَةٍ تُجْزَىٰٓ ۝ إِلَّا ٱبْتِغَآءَ وَجْهِ رَبِّهِ ٱلْأَعْلَىٰ ۝ وَلَسَوْفَ يَرْضَىٰ ۝

سُورَةُ الضُّحَى

بِسْمِ ٱللَّهِ ٱلرَّحْمَٰنِ ٱلرَّحِيمِ

وَٱلضُّحَىٰ ۝ وَٱلَّيْلِ إِذَا سَجَىٰ ۝ مَا وَدَّعَكَ رَبُّكَ وَمَا قَلَىٰ ۝ وَلَلْءَاخِرَةُ خَيْرٌ لَّكَ مِنَ ٱلْأُولَىٰ ۝ وَلَسَوْفَ يُعْطِيكَ رَبُّكَ فَتَرْضَىٰٓ ۝ أَلَمْ يَجِدْكَ يَتِيمًا فَـَٔاوَىٰ ۝ وَوَجَدَكَ ضَآلًّا فَهَدَىٰ ۝ وَوَجَدَكَ عَآئِلًا فَأَغْنَىٰ ۝ فَأَمَّا ٱلْيَتِيمَ فَلَا تَقْهَرْ ۝ وَأَمَّا ٱلسَّآئِلَ فَلَا تَنْهَرْ ۝ وَأَمَّا بِنِعْمَةِ رَبِّكَ فَحَدِّثْ ۝

سُورَةُ الشَّرْحِ

بِسْمِ ٱللَّهِ ٱلرَّحْمَٰنِ ٱلرَّحِيمِ

أَلَمْ نَشْرَحْ لَكَ صَدْرَكَ ۝ وَوَضَعْنَا عَنكَ وِزْرَكَ ۝

My Juz' 'Amma Journey

Write down as many examples as you can from the page:

Identify Makharij of 6 letters	Ghunnah	Madd	Elevated sounds
_____	_____	_____	_____

Noon Saakin & Tanween
Idgham: _____
Ikhfaa': _____
Iqlab: _____

Meem Saakin
Idgham: _____
Ikhfaa': _____

Qalqalah
_____

Hamzatul-wasl
_____

My Juz' 'Amma Journey

4. And raised high your fame?

5, 6. So verily, with the hardship, there is relief, verily, with the hardship, there is relief.

7, 8. So when you have finished from your occupation, then stand up for prayer. And to your Lord Alone turn in all your intentions, hopes and invocations.

Surah at-Teen shows that our value is in how strong we are in religion. That is why Allah takes an oath on the places of revelation in the first three verses.

1-3. By the fig, and the olive (in Palestine). By Mount Sinai (in Egypt). And by this city of security (Makkah).

4. Verily, We created man of the best stature.

5. Then We reduced him to the lowest of the low,

6. Except those who believe and do righteous deeds, then they shall have an endless reward in Paradise.

7, 8. Then what or who causes you, O disbelievers, to deny the Resurrection? Is not Allah the Best of judges?

Surah al-Alaq highlights the perfection of the human through revelation and encourages him to submit himself to his Lord.

1-5. Read! In the Name of your Lord, Who has created. He has created man miraculously from a clot of blood. Read! And your Lord is the Most Generous, Who has taught by the pen. He has taught man that which he did not know.

6, 7. Nay! Verily, man transgresses all bounds in disbelief because he considers himself self-sufficient.

8. Surely! To your Lord is the return.

9, 10. Have you O Messenger seen Abu Jahl who prevents you to pray?

11, 12. What if the Messenger was on the guidance of Allah or enjoining righteousness?

65

الْجُزْءُ الثَّلَاثُونَ   سُورَةُ التِّينِ

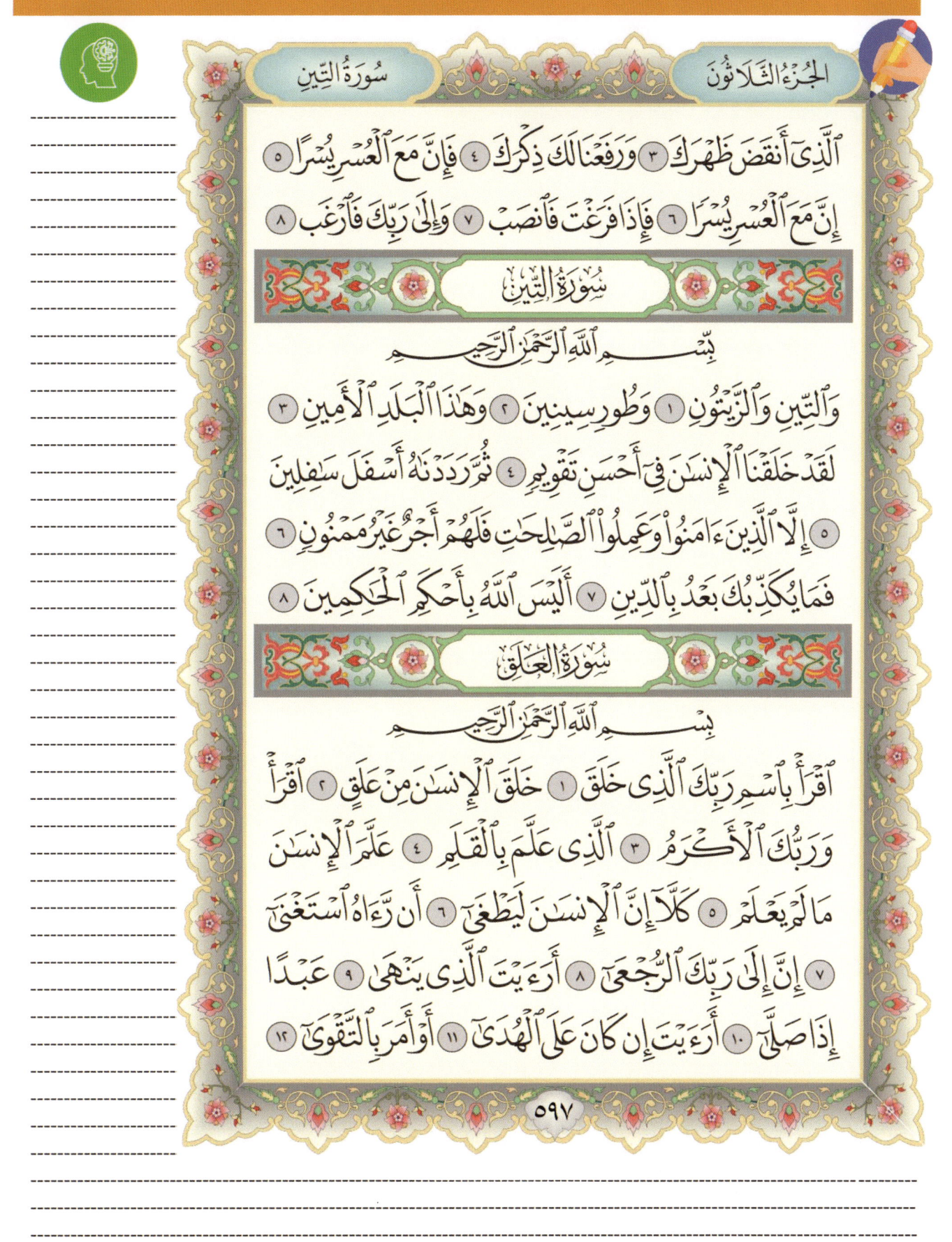

ٱلَّذِىٓ أَنقَضَ ظَهْرَكَ ۝٣ وَرَفَعْنَا لَكَ ذِكْرَكَ ۝٤ فَإِنَّ مَعَ ٱلْعُسْرِ يُسْرًا ۝٥ إِنَّ مَعَ ٱلْعُسْرِ يُسْرًا ۝٦ فَإِذَا فَرَغْتَ فَٱنصَبْ ۝٧ وَإِلَىٰ رَبِّكَ فَٱرْغَب ۝٨

سُورَةُ التِّينِ

بِسْمِ ٱللَّهِ ٱلرَّحْمَٰنِ ٱلرَّحِيمِ

وَٱلتِّينِ وَٱلزَّيْتُونِ ۝١ وَطُورِ سِينِينَ ۝٢ وَهَٰذَا ٱلْبَلَدِ ٱلْأَمِينِ ۝٣ لَقَدْ خَلَقْنَا ٱلْإِنسَٰنَ فِىٓ أَحْسَنِ تَقْوِيمٍ ۝٤ ثُمَّ رَدَدْنَٰهُ أَسْفَلَ سَٰفِلِينَ ۝٥ إِلَّا ٱلَّذِينَ ءَامَنُوا۟ وَعَمِلُوا۟ ٱلصَّٰلِحَٰتِ فَلَهُمْ أَجْرٌ غَيْرُ مَمْنُونٍ ۝٦ فَمَا يُكَذِّبُكَ بَعْدُ بِٱلدِّينِ ۝٧ أَلَيْسَ ٱللَّهُ بِأَحْكَمِ ٱلْحَٰكِمِينَ ۝٨

سُورَةُ الْعَلَقِ

بِسْمِ ٱللَّهِ ٱلرَّحْمَٰنِ ٱلرَّحِيمِ

ٱقْرَأْ بِٱسْمِ رَبِّكَ ٱلَّذِى خَلَقَ ۝١ خَلَقَ ٱلْإِنسَٰنَ مِنْ عَلَقٍ ۝٢ ٱقْرَأْ وَرَبُّكَ ٱلْأَكْرَمُ ۝٣ ٱلَّذِى عَلَّمَ بِٱلْقَلَمِ ۝٤ عَلَّمَ ٱلْإِنسَٰنَ مَا لَمْ يَعْلَمْ ۝٥ كَلَّآ إِنَّ ٱلْإِنسَٰنَ لَيَطْغَىٰٓ ۝٦ أَن رَّءَاهُ ٱسْتَغْنَىٰٓ ۝٧ إِنَّ إِلَىٰ رَبِّكَ ٱلرُّجْعَىٰٓ ۝٨ أَرَءَيْتَ ٱلَّذِى يَنْهَىٰ ۝٩ عَبْدًا إِذَا صَلَّىٰٓ ۝١٠ أَرَءَيْتَ إِن كَانَ عَلَى ٱلْهُدَىٰٓ ۝١١ أَوْ أَمَرَ بِٱلتَّقْوَىٰٓ ۝١٢

٥٩٧

My Juz' 'Amma Journey

Write down as many examples as you can from the page:

Identify Makharij of 6 letters	Ghunnah	Madd	Elevated sounds

Noon Saakin & Tanween	Meem Saakin	Qalqalah	Hamzatul-wasl
Idgham: -------	Idgham: -------		
Ikhfaa': -------	Ikhfaa': -------		
Iqlab: -------			

67

الجزء الثلاثون سورة التين

ٱلَّذِىٓ أَنقَضَ ظَهْرَكَ ۝ وَرَفَعْنَا لَكَ ذِكْرَكَ ۝ فَإِنَّ مَعَ ٱلْعُسْرِ يُسْرًا ۝ إِنَّ مَعَ ٱلْعُسْرِ يُسْرًا ۝ فَإِذَا فَرَغْتَ فَٱنصَبْ ۝ وَإِلَىٰ رَبِّكَ فَٱرْغَب ۝

سورة التين

بِسْمِ ٱللَّهِ ٱلرَّحْمَٰنِ ٱلرَّحِيمِ

وَٱلتِّينِ وَٱلزَّيْتُونِ ۝ وَطُورِ سِينِينَ ۝ وَهَٰذَا ٱلْبَلَدِ ٱلْأَمِينِ ۝ لَقَدْ خَلَقْنَا ٱلْإِنسَٰنَ فِىٓ أَحْسَنِ تَقْوِيمٍ ۝ ثُمَّ رَدَدْنَٰهُ أَسْفَلَ سَٰفِلِينَ ۝ إِلَّا ٱلَّذِينَ ءَامَنُوا۟ وَعَمِلُوا۟ ٱلصَّٰلِحَٰتِ فَلَهُمْ أَجْرٌ غَيْرُ مَمْنُونٍ ۝ فَمَا يُكَذِّبُكَ بَعْدُ بِٱلدِّينِ ۝ أَلَيْسَ ٱللَّهُ بِأَحْكَمِ ٱلْحَٰكِمِينَ ۝

سورة العلق

بِسْمِ ٱللَّهِ ٱلرَّحْمَٰنِ ٱلرَّحِيمِ

ٱقْرَأْ بِٱسْمِ رَبِّكَ ٱلَّذِى خَلَقَ ۝ خَلَقَ ٱلْإِنسَٰنَ مِنْ عَلَقٍ ۝ ٱقْرَأْ وَرَبُّكَ ٱلْأَكْرَمُ ۝ ٱلَّذِى عَلَّمَ بِٱلْقَلَمِ ۝ عَلَّمَ ٱلْإِنسَٰنَ مَا لَمْ يَعْلَمْ ۝ كَلَّآ إِنَّ ٱلْإِنسَٰنَ لَيَطْغَىٰٓ ۝ أَن رَّءَاهُ ٱسْتَغْنَىٰٓ ۝ إِنَّ إِلَىٰ رَبِّكَ ٱلرُّجْعَىٰٓ ۝ أَرَءَيْتَ ٱلَّذِى يَنْهَىٰ ۝ عَبْدًا إِذَا صَلَّىٰٓ ۝ أَرَءَيْتَ إِن كَانَ عَلَى ٱلْهُدَىٰٓ ۝ أَوْ أَمَرَ بِٱلتَّقْوَىٰٓ ۝

٥٩٧

الجزء الثلاثون ۝ سورة القدر

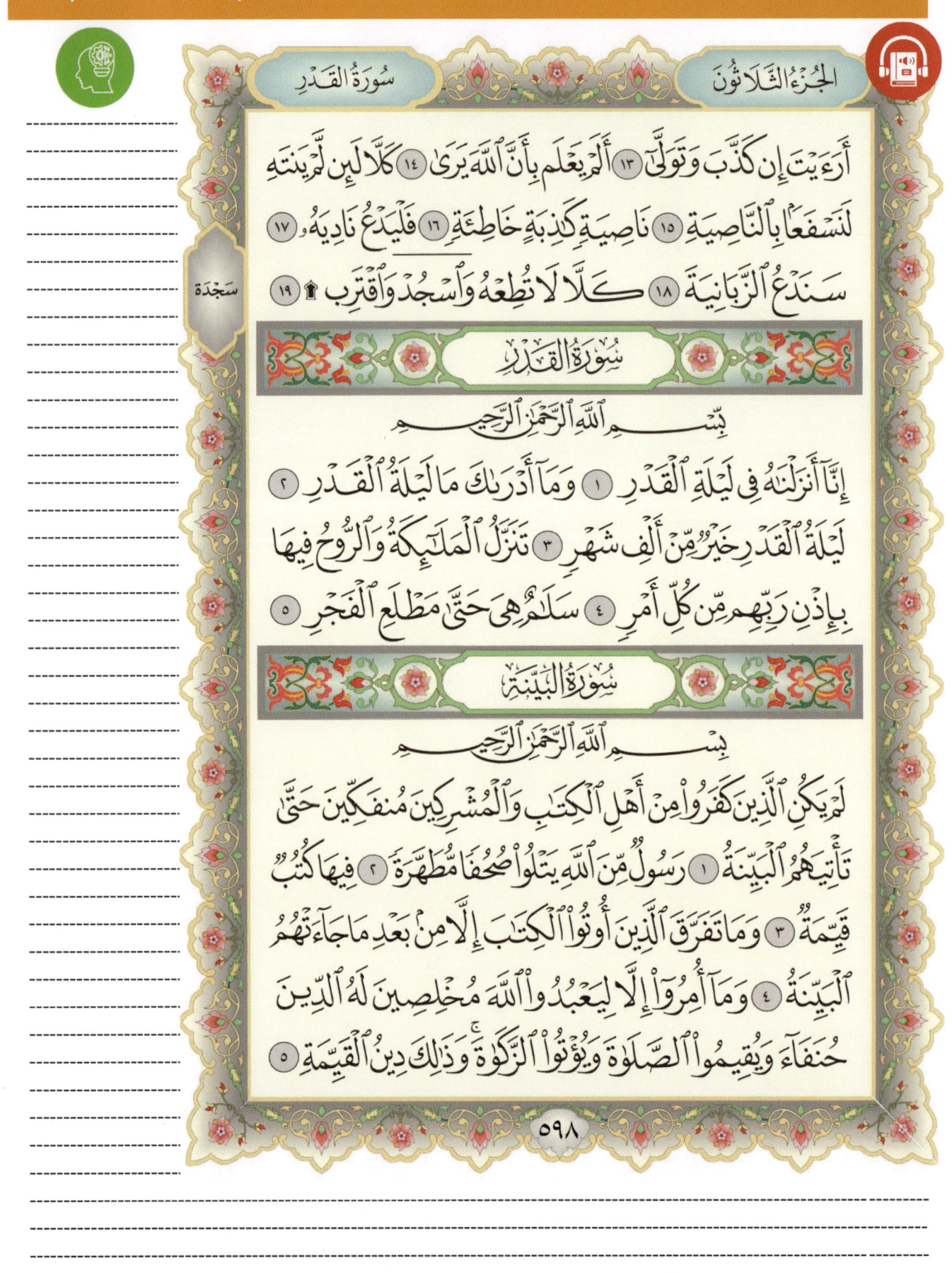

أَرَأَيْتَ إِن كَذَّبَ وَتَوَلَّىٰ ۝ أَلَمْ يَعْلَم بِأَنَّ ٱللَّهَ يَرَىٰ ۝ كَلَّا لَئِن لَّمْ يَنتَهِ لَنَسْفَعًۢا بِٱلنَّاصِيَةِ ۝ نَاصِيَةٍ كَاذِبَةٍ خَاطِئَةٍ ۝ فَلْيَدْعُ نَادِيَهُۥ ۝ سَنَدْعُ ٱلزَّبَانِيَةَ ۝ كَلَّا لَا تُطِعْهُ وَٱسْجُدْ وَٱقْتَرِب ۩ ۝

سجدة

سُورَةُ ٱلْقَدْرِ

بِسْمِ ٱللَّهِ ٱلرَّحْمَٰنِ ٱلرَّحِيمِ

إِنَّآ أَنزَلْنَٰهُ فِى لَيْلَةِ ٱلْقَدْرِ ۝ وَمَآ أَدْرَىٰكَ مَا لَيْلَةُ ٱلْقَدْرِ ۝ لَيْلَةُ ٱلْقَدْرِ خَيْرٌ مِّنْ أَلْفِ شَهْرٍ ۝ تَنَزَّلُ ٱلْمَلَٰٓئِكَةُ وَٱلرُّوحُ فِيهَا بِإِذْنِ رَبِّهِم مِّن كُلِّ أَمْرٍ ۝ سَلَٰمٌ هِىَ حَتَّىٰ مَطْلَعِ ٱلْفَجْرِ ۝

سُورَةُ ٱلْبَيِّنَةِ

بِسْمِ ٱللَّهِ ٱلرَّحْمَٰنِ ٱلرَّحِيمِ

لَمْ يَكُنِ ٱلَّذِينَ كَفَرُوا۟ مِنْ أَهْلِ ٱلْكِتَٰبِ وَٱلْمُشْرِكِينَ مُنفَكِّينَ حَتَّىٰ تَأْتِيَهُمُ ٱلْبَيِّنَةُ ۝ رَسُولٌ مِّنَ ٱللَّهِ يَتْلُوا۟ صُحُفًا مُّطَهَّرَةً ۝ فِيهَا كُتُبٌ قَيِّمَةٌ ۝ وَمَا تَفَرَّقَ ٱلَّذِينَ أُوتُوا۟ ٱلْكِتَٰبَ إِلَّا مِنۢ بَعْدِ مَا جَآءَتْهُمُ ٱلْبَيِّنَةُ ۝ وَمَآ أُمِرُوٓا۟ إِلَّا لِيَعْبُدُوا۟ ٱللَّهَ مُخْلِصِينَ لَهُ ٱلدِّينَ حُنَفَآءَ وَيُقِيمُوا۟ ٱلصَّلَوٰةَ وَيُؤْتُوا۟ ٱلزَّكَوٰةَ ۚ وَذَٰلِكَ دِينُ ٱلْقَيِّمَةِ ۝

٥٩٨

My Juz' 'Amma Journey

13, 14. What if the disbeliever denies the Qur'an and turns away? Does he not know that Allah sees what he does?

15, 16. Nay! If he does not stop, We will catch him by his lying and sinful forelock!

17, 18. Then, let him call upon his helpers, and We will call the guards of Hell!

19. Nay! O Messenger do not obey him. Fall prostrate and draw near to Allah!

Surah al-Qadr highlights the greatness of the Night of Decree, its virtue and what was revealed on it.

1, 2. Verily! We have sent the whole Qur'an down in the night of al-Qadr. Do you know what the night of al-Qadr is?

3. The night of al-Qadr is better than a thousand months.

4. In it, the angels and the Ruh, angel Jibreel, descend by Allah's Permission with all Decrees.

5. It is peace until the appearance of dawn.

Surah al-Bayyinah focuses on the value of the Message of Prophet Muhammad ﷺ, its clarity and perfection.

1. The disbelieving Jews, Christians and idol worshippers were not going to leave their disbelief until there came to them clear evidence.

2, 3. A Messenger from Allah, reciting purified sheets of the Qur'an, which contain correct and straight laws from Allah.

4. And the Jews, Christians denied the truth only after there came to them clear evidence.

5. And they were only commanded to sincerely worship Allah, perform Salah and give Zakah. And this is the right religion.

الجزءُ الثَّلاثونَ سُورَةُ القَدْرِ

أَرَءَيْتَ إِن كَذَّبَ وَتَوَلَّىٰ ۝ أَلَمْ يَعْلَم بِأَنَّ ٱللَّهَ يَرَىٰ ۝ كَلَّا لَئِن لَّمْ يَنتَهِ لَنَسْفَعًۢا بِٱلنَّاصِيَةِ ۝ نَاصِيَةٍ كَٰذِبَةٍ خَاطِئَةٍ ۝ فَلْيَدْعُ نَادِيَهُۥ ۝ سَنَدْعُ ٱلزَّبَانِيَةَ ۝ كَلَّا لَا تُطِعْهُ وَٱسْجُدْ وَٱقْتَرِب ۩ ۝

سَجْدَة

سُورَةُ القَدْرِ

بِسْمِ ٱللَّهِ ٱلرَّحْمَٰنِ ٱلرَّحِيمِ

إِنَّآ أَنزَلْنَٰهُ فِى لَيْلَةِ ٱلْقَدْرِ ۝ وَمَآ أَدْرَىٰكَ مَا لَيْلَةُ ٱلْقَدْرِ ۝ لَيْلَةُ ٱلْقَدْرِ خَيْرٌ مِّنْ أَلْفِ شَهْرٍ ۝ تَنَزَّلُ ٱلْمَلَٰٓئِكَةُ وَٱلرُّوحُ فِيهَا بِإِذْنِ رَبِّهِم مِّن كُلِّ أَمْرٍ ۝ سَلَٰمٌ هِىَ حَتَّىٰ مَطْلَعِ ٱلْفَجْرِ ۝

سُورَةُ البَيِّنَةِ

بِسْمِ ٱللَّهِ ٱلرَّحْمَٰنِ ٱلرَّحِيمِ

لَمْ يَكُنِ ٱلَّذِينَ كَفَرُوا۟ مِنْ أَهْلِ ٱلْكِتَٰبِ وَٱلْمُشْرِكِينَ مُنفَكِّينَ حَتَّىٰ تَأْتِيَهُمُ ٱلْبَيِّنَةُ ۝ رَسُولٌ مِّنَ ٱللَّهِ يَتْلُوا۟ صُحُفًا مُّطَهَّرَةً ۝ فِيهَا كُتُبٌ قَيِّمَةٌ ۝ وَمَا تَفَرَّقَ ٱلَّذِينَ أُوتُوا۟ ٱلْكِتَٰبَ إِلَّا مِنۢ بَعْدِ مَا جَآءَتْهُمُ ٱلْبَيِّنَةُ ۝ وَمَآ أُمِرُوٓا۟ إِلَّا لِيَعْبُدُوا۟ ٱللَّهَ مُخْلِصِينَ لَهُ ٱلدِّينَ حُنَفَآءَ وَيُقِيمُوا۟ ٱلصَّلَوٰةَ وَيُؤْتُوا۟ ٱلزَّكَوٰةَ ۚ وَذَٰلِكَ دِينُ ٱلْقَيِّمَةِ ۝

٥٩٨

My Juz' 'Amma Journey

Write down as many examples as you can from the page:

Identify Makharij of 6 letters	Ghunnah	Madd	Elevated sounds

Noon Saakin & Tanween	Meem Saakin	Qalqalah	Hamzatul-wasl
Idgham: Ikhfaa': Iqlab:	Idgham: Ikhfaa':		

My Juz' 'Amma Journey

6. Verily, the disbelieving Jews, Christians and idol worshippers will be in Hell forever. They are the worst of creatures.

7. Verily, those who believe and do righteous good deeds are the best of creatures.

8. Their reward with their Lord is Gardens of Eternity, underneath which rivers flow. They will be there forever. Allah is Well-Pleased with them, and they are well-pleased with Him. This is the reward for him who fears his Lord.

Surah az-Zalzalah awakens the neglectful hearts so that they remember the detailed questioning they will go through on the day of Judgement.

1. When the earth is shaken with its final earthquake,

2. And when the earth throws out its burdens of dead people for resurrection,

3. And when man will say: "What is the matter with it?",

4, 5. Then, the earth will declare that Day its news about all what happened over it of good or evil, because your Lord has inspired it.

6. That Day mankind will come in split groups so that they may be shown their deeds.

7, 8. So whosoever does good equal to the weight of an atom shall see it. And whosoever does evil equal to the weight of an atom shall see it.

Surah al-'Adiyat mentions the reality of man in his interest in the worldly affairs, reminding him of his definite return, and encouraging him to fix his way.

1-5. Allah swears by the horses that run, with panting breath, striking sparks of fire by their hooves, raiding at dawn, stirring up clouds of dust and penetrating into the midst of the enemy.

الجزء الثلاثون — سُورَةُ الزَّلْزَلَةِ

إِنَّ ٱلَّذِينَ كَفَرُوا۟ مِنْ أَهْلِ ٱلْكِتَٰبِ وَٱلْمُشْرِكِينَ فِى نَارِ جَهَنَّمَ خَٰلِدِينَ فِيهَآ ۚ أُو۟لَٰٓئِكَ هُمْ شَرُّ ٱلْبَرِيَّةِ ﴿٦﴾ إِنَّ ٱلَّذِينَ ءَامَنُوا۟ وَعَمِلُوا۟ ٱلصَّٰلِحَٰتِ أُو۟لَٰٓئِكَ هُمْ خَيْرُ ٱلْبَرِيَّةِ ﴿٧﴾ جَزَآؤُهُمْ عِندَ رَبِّهِمْ جَنَّٰتُ عَدْنٍ تَجْرِى مِن تَحْتِهَا ٱلْأَنْهَٰرُ خَٰلِدِينَ فِيهَآ أَبَدًا ۖ رَّضِىَ ٱللَّهُ عَنْهُمْ وَرَضُوا۟ عَنْهُ ۚ ذَٰلِكَ لِمَنْ خَشِىَ رَبَّهُۥ ﴿٨﴾

سُورَةُ الزَّلْزَلَةِ

بِسْمِ ٱللَّهِ ٱلرَّحْمَٰنِ ٱلرَّحِيمِ

إِذَا زُلْزِلَتِ ٱلْأَرْضُ زِلْزَالَهَا ﴿١﴾ وَأَخْرَجَتِ ٱلْأَرْضُ أَثْقَالَهَا ﴿٢﴾ وَقَالَ ٱلْإِنسَٰنُ مَا لَهَا ﴿٣﴾ يَوْمَئِذٍ تُحَدِّثُ أَخْبَارَهَا ﴿٤﴾ بِأَنَّ رَبَّكَ أَوْحَىٰ لَهَا ﴿٥﴾ يَوْمَئِذٍ يَصْدُرُ ٱلنَّاسُ أَشْتَاتًا لِّيُرَوْا۟ أَعْمَٰلَهُمْ ﴿٦﴾ فَمَن يَعْمَلْ مِثْقَالَ ذَرَّةٍ خَيْرًا يَرَهُۥ ﴿٧﴾ وَمَن يَعْمَلْ مِثْقَالَ ذَرَّةٍ شَرًّا يَرَهُۥ ﴿٨﴾

سُورَةُ الْعَادِيَاتِ

بِسْمِ ٱللَّهِ ٱلرَّحْمَٰنِ ٱلرَّحِيمِ

وَٱلْعَٰدِيَٰتِ ضَبْحًا ﴿١﴾ فَٱلْمُورِيَٰتِ قَدْحًا ﴿٢﴾ فَٱلْمُغِيرَٰتِ صُبْحًا ﴿٣﴾ فَأَثَرْنَ بِهِۦ نَقْعًا ﴿٤﴾ فَوَسَطْنَ بِهِۦ جَمْعًا ﴿٥﴾

٥٩٩

My Juz' 'Amma Journey

Write down as many examples as you can from the page:

Identify Makharij of 6 letters	Ghunnah	Madd	Elevated sounds

Noon Saakin & Tanween
Idgham: ----------------
Ikhfaa': ----------------
Iqlab: ----------------

Meem Saakin
Idgham: ----------------
Ikhfaa': ----------------

Qalqalah

Hamzatul-wasl

75

الجزء الثلاثون سورة الزلزلة

إِنَّ ٱلَّذِينَ كَفَرُوا۟ مِنْ أَهْلِ ٱلْكِتَـٰبِ وَٱلْمُشْرِكِينَ فِى نَارِ جَهَنَّمَ خَـٰلِدِينَ فِيهَآ ۚ أُو۟لَـٰٓئِكَ هُمْ شَرُّ ٱلْبَرِيَّةِ ۝ إِنَّ ٱلَّذِينَ ءَامَنُوا۟ وَعَمِلُوا۟ ٱلصَّـٰلِحَـٰتِ أُو۟لَـٰٓئِكَ هُمْ خَيْرُ ٱلْبَرِيَّةِ ۝ جَزَآؤُهُمْ عِندَ رَبِّهِمْ جَنَّـٰتُ عَدْنٍ تَجْرِى مِن تَحْتِهَا ٱلْأَنْهَـٰرُ خَـٰلِدِينَ فِيهَآ أَبَدًا ۖ رَّضِىَ ٱللَّهُ عَنْهُمْ وَرَضُوا۟ عَنْهُ ۚ ذَٰلِكَ لِمَنْ خَشِىَ رَبَّهُۥ ۝

سورة الزلزلة

بِسْمِ ٱللَّهِ ٱلرَّحْمَـٰنِ ٱلرَّحِيمِ

إِذَا زُلْزِلَتِ ٱلْأَرْضُ زِلْزَالَهَا ۝ وَأَخْرَجَتِ ٱلْأَرْضُ أَثْقَالَهَا ۝ وَقَالَ ٱلْإِنسَـٰنُ مَا لَهَا ۝ يَوْمَئِذٍ تُحَدِّثُ أَخْبَارَهَا ۝ بِأَنَّ رَبَّكَ أَوْحَىٰ لَهَا ۝ يَوْمَئِذٍ يَصْدُرُ ٱلنَّاسُ أَشْتَاتًا لِّيُرَوْا۟ أَعْمَـٰلَهُمْ ۝ فَمَن يَعْمَلْ مِثْقَالَ ذَرَّةٍ خَيْرًا يَرَهُۥ ۝ وَمَن يَعْمَلْ مِثْقَالَ ذَرَّةٍ شَرًّا يَرَهُۥ ۝

سورة العاديات

بِسْمِ ٱللَّهِ ٱلرَّحْمَـٰنِ ٱلرَّحِيمِ

وَٱلْعَـٰدِيَـٰتِ ضَبْحًا ۝ فَٱلْمُورِيَـٰتِ قَدْحًا ۝ فَٱلْمُغِيرَٰتِ صُبْحًا ۝ فَأَثَرْنَ بِهِۦ نَقْعًا ۝ فَوَسَطْنَ بِهِۦ جَمْعًا ۝

٥٩٩

الجزء الثلاثون — سُورَةُ الْقَارِعَةِ

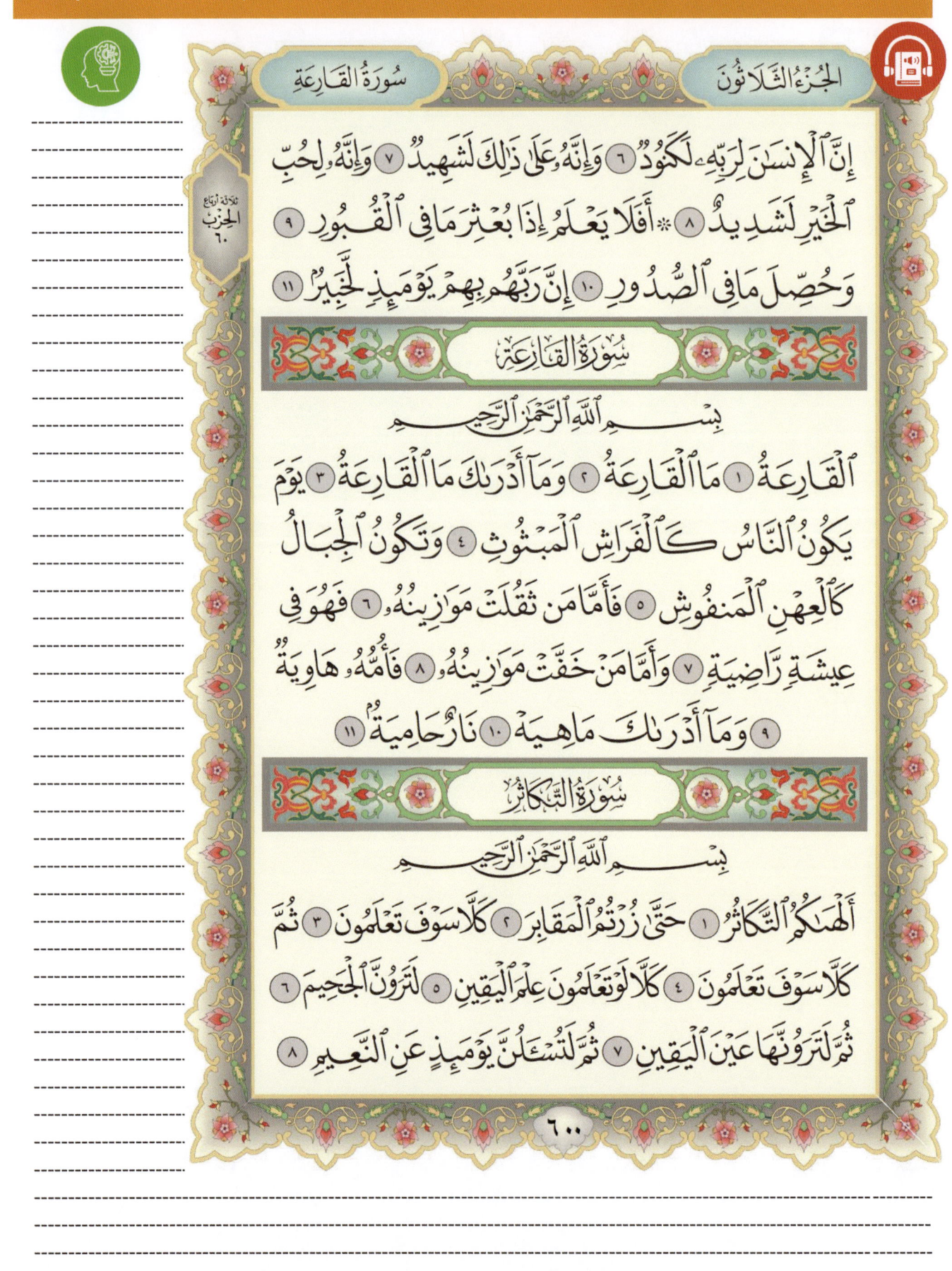

إِنَّ الْإِنسَانَ لِرَبِّهِ لَكَنُودٌ ۝٦ وَإِنَّهُ عَلَىٰ ذَٰلِكَ لَشَهِيدٌ ۝٧ وَإِنَّهُ لِحُبِّ الْخَيْرِ لَشَدِيدٌ ۝٨ ۞ أَفَلَا يَعْلَمُ إِذَا بُعْثِرَ مَا فِي الْقُبُورِ ۝٩ وَحُصِّلَ مَا فِي الصُّدُورِ ۝١٠ إِنَّ رَبَّهُم بِهِمْ يَوْمَئِذٍ لَّخَبِيرٌ ۝١١

ثلاثة أرباع الحزب ٦٠

سُورَةُ الْقَارِعَةِ

بِسْمِ اللَّهِ الرَّحْمَٰنِ الرَّحِيمِ

الْقَارِعَةُ ۝١ مَا الْقَارِعَةُ ۝٢ وَمَا أَدْرَاكَ مَا الْقَارِعَةُ ۝٣ يَوْمَ يَكُونُ النَّاسُ كَالْفَرَاشِ الْمَبْثُوثِ ۝٤ وَتَكُونُ الْجِبَالُ كَالْعِهْنِ الْمَنفُوشِ ۝٥ فَأَمَّا مَن ثَقُلَتْ مَوَازِينُهُ ۝٦ فَهُوَ فِي عِيشَةٍ رَّاضِيَةٍ ۝٧ وَأَمَّا مَنْ خَفَّتْ مَوَازِينُهُ ۝٨ فَأُمُّهُ هَاوِيَةٌ ۝٩ وَمَا أَدْرَاكَ مَا هِيَهْ ۝١٠ نَارٌ حَامِيَةٌ ۝١١

سُورَةُ التَّكَاثُرِ

بِسْمِ اللَّهِ الرَّحْمَٰنِ الرَّحِيمِ

أَلْهَاكُمُ التَّكَاثُرُ ۝١ حَتَّىٰ زُرْتُمُ الْمَقَابِرَ ۝٢ كَلَّا سَوْفَ تَعْلَمُونَ ۝٣ ثُمَّ كَلَّا سَوْفَ تَعْلَمُونَ ۝٤ كَلَّا لَوْ تَعْلَمُونَ عِلْمَ الْيَقِينِ ۝٥ لَتَرَوُنَّ الْجَحِيمَ ۝٦ ثُمَّ لَتَرَوُنَّهَا عَيْنَ الْيَقِينِ ۝٧ ثُمَّ لَتُسْأَلُنَّ يَوْمَئِذٍ عَنِ النَّعِيمِ ۝٨

٦٠٠

My Juz' 'Amma Journey

6. Verily, the disbelieving man is ungrateful to his Lord;

7. And he bears witness to this fact by his deeds.

8. And verily, he loves wealth badly.

9. Does not he know that when all mankind is resurrected,

10. And when all that which is in the breasts shall be made known,

11. They, then, will realize that Day that their Lord is indeed Well-Aware with them.

Surah al-Qari'ah strikes the hearts so that we remember the horrors of the Day of Judgement

1-3. The striking Hour of the Day of Resurrection, do you know what it is?

4. It is a Day when mankind will be like moths scattered about,

5. And the mountains will be like carded wool,

6, 7. Then as for him whose balance of good deeds will be heavy, he will live a pleasant life in Paradise.

8-11. But as for him whose balance of good deeds will be light, he will have his home in Hell. Do you know what Hell is? It is a hot blazing Fire!

Surah at-Takathur reminds those busy with this world of death and accountability. It is also known as the Surah of the businessmen.

1. The mutual competition for the piling up of worldly things distracts you,

2. Until you die and go to the graves.

3, 4. Nay! You shall come to know!

5-7. Nay! If you know with certainty the result of being busy with piling up, you would see the blazing Fire. And indeed, you shall certainty see it with your eyes!

8. Then, on that Day, you shall be asked about all delight you enjoyed in the first world.

My Juz' 'Amma Journey

الجزءُ الثَّلاثُونَ سُورَةُ القَارِعَة

إِنَّ ٱلْإِنسَٰنَ لِرَبِّهِۦ لَكَنُودٌ ۝ وَإِنَّهُۥ عَلَىٰ ذَٰلِكَ لَشَهِيدٌ ۝ وَإِنَّهُۥ لِحُبِّ ٱلْخَيْرِ لَشَدِيدٌ ۝ ۞ أَفَلَا يَعْلَمُ إِذَا بُعْثِرَ مَا فِى ٱلْقُبُورِ ۝ وَحُصِّلَ مَا فِى ٱلصُّدُورِ ۝ إِنَّ رَبَّهُم بِهِمْ يَوْمَئِذٍ لَّخَبِيرٌۢ ۝

سُورَةُ القَارِعَة

بِسْمِ ٱللَّهِ ٱلرَّحْمَٰنِ ٱلرَّحِيمِ

ٱلْقَارِعَةُ ۝ مَا ٱلْقَارِعَةُ ۝ وَمَآ أَدْرَىٰكَ مَا ٱلْقَارِعَةُ ۝ يَوْمَ يَكُونُ ٱلنَّاسُ كَٱلْفَرَاشِ ٱلْمَبْثُوثِ ۝ وَتَكُونُ ٱلْجِبَالُ كَٱلْعِهْنِ ٱلْمَنفُوشِ ۝ فَأَمَّا مَن ثَقُلَتْ مَوَٰزِينُهُۥ ۝ فَهُوَ فِى عِيشَةٍ رَّاضِيَةٍ ۝ وَأَمَّا مَنْ خَفَّتْ مَوَٰزِينُهُۥ ۝ فَأُمُّهُۥ هَاوِيَةٌ ۝ وَمَآ أَدْرَىٰكَ مَا هِيَهْ ۝ نَارٌ حَامِيَةٌۢ ۝

سُورَةُ التَّكَاثُر

بِسْمِ ٱللَّهِ ٱلرَّحْمَٰنِ ٱلرَّحِيمِ

أَلْهَىٰكُمُ ٱلتَّكَاثُرُ ۝ حَتَّىٰ زُرْتُمُ ٱلْمَقَابِرَ ۝ كَلَّا سَوْفَ تَعْلَمُونَ ۝ ثُمَّ كَلَّا سَوْفَ تَعْلَمُونَ ۝ كَلَّا لَوْ تَعْلَمُونَ عِلْمَ ٱلْيَقِينِ ۝ لَتَرَوُنَّ ٱلْجَحِيمَ ۝ ثُمَّ لَتَرَوُنَّهَا عَيْنَ ٱلْيَقِينِ ۝ ثُمَّ لَتُسْـَٔلُنَّ يَوْمَئِذٍ عَنِ ٱلنَّعِيمِ ۝

My Juz' 'Amma Journey

Write down as many examples as you can from the page:

Identify Makharij of 6 letters	Ghunnah	Madd	Elevated sounds

Noon Saakin & Tanween	Meem Saakin	Qalqalah	Hamzatul-wasl
Idgham:	Idgham:		
Ikhfaa':	Ikhfaa':		
Iqlab:			

My Juz' 'Amma Journey

Surah al-Asr mentions the reality of gain and loss in life, pointing out the value of time.

1. By the time,	2. Man is in loss,

3. Except those who believe, do good deeds, recommend one another to the truth and recommend one another to patience.

Surah al-Humazah warns those who are arrogant and keep mocking the religion and the religious people.

1. Woe to every slanderer and backbiter.

2, 3. He who collects wealth and greedily counts it, thinking that it will make him last forever!

4-7. Nay! He will be thrown into the crushing Fire. It is a kindled fire from Allah leaping up over the hearts.

8, 9. This Fire shall be closed in on them, and they will be stretched forth on pillars.

Surah al-Feel shows Allah's Power in protecting His Sacred House.

1. Did you know how your Lord dealt with the people of the Elephant, who came in an army of elephants to destroy the Ka'bah?

2. Did not He make their plan get lost?

3, 4. And sent against them birds in flocks, striking them with stones of clay.

5. And made them into ashes like corn that has been eaten up by cattle.

الجزءُ الثَلاثُونَ — سُورَةُ العَصْرِ

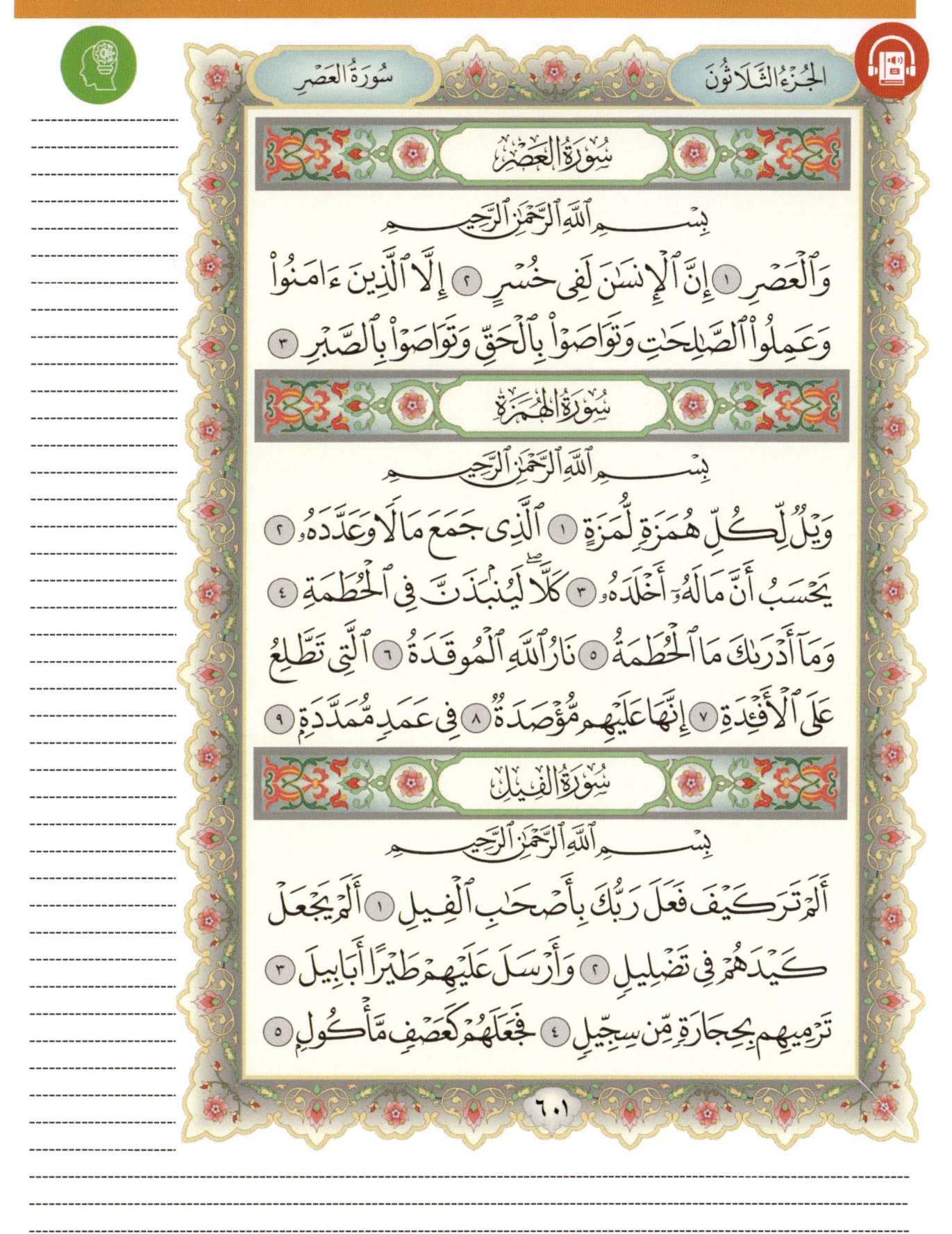

سُورَةُ العَصْرِ

بِسْمِ اللَّهِ الرَّحْمَٰنِ الرَّحِيمِ

وَالْعَصْرِ ﴿١﴾ إِنَّ الْإِنسَانَ لَفِي خُسْرٍ ﴿٢﴾ إِلَّا الَّذِينَ آمَنُوا وَعَمِلُوا الصَّالِحَاتِ وَتَوَاصَوْا بِالْحَقِّ وَتَوَاصَوْا بِالصَّبْرِ ﴿٣﴾

سُورَةُ الهُمَزَةِ

بِسْمِ اللَّهِ الرَّحْمَٰنِ الرَّحِيمِ

وَيْلٌ لِّكُلِّ هُمَزَةٍ لُّمَزَةٍ ﴿١﴾ الَّذِي جَمَعَ مَالًا وَعَدَّدَهُ ﴿٢﴾ يَحْسَبُ أَنَّ مَالَهُ أَخْلَدَهُ ﴿٣﴾ كَلَّا ۖ لَيُنبَذَنَّ فِي الْحُطَمَةِ ﴿٤﴾ وَمَا أَدْرَاكَ مَا الْحُطَمَةُ ﴿٥﴾ نَارُ اللَّهِ الْمُوقَدَةُ ﴿٦﴾ الَّتِي تَطَّلِعُ عَلَى الْأَفْئِدَةِ ﴿٧﴾ إِنَّهَا عَلَيْهِم مُّؤْصَدَةٌ ﴿٨﴾ فِي عَمَدٍ مُّمَدَّدَةٍ ﴿٩﴾

سُورَةُ الفِيلِ

بِسْمِ اللَّهِ الرَّحْمَٰنِ الرَّحِيمِ

أَلَمْ تَرَ كَيْفَ فَعَلَ رَبُّكَ بِأَصْحَابِ الْفِيلِ ﴿١﴾ أَلَمْ يَجْعَلْ كَيْدَهُمْ فِي تَضْلِيلٍ ﴿٢﴾ وَأَرْسَلَ عَلَيْهِمْ طَيْرًا أَبَابِيلَ ﴿٣﴾ تَرْمِيهِم بِحِجَارَةٍ مِّن سِجِّيلٍ ﴿٤﴾ فَجَعَلَهُمْ كَعَصْفٍ مَّأْكُولٍ ﴿٥﴾

٦٠١

My Juz' 'Amma Journey

Write down as many examples as you can from the page:

Identify Makharij of 6 letters	Ghunnah	Madd	Elevated sounds

Noon Saakin & Tanween
Idgham: --------------------------
Ikhfaa': --------------------------
Iqlab: --------------------------

Meem Saakin
Idgham: --------------------------
Ikhfaa': --------------------------

Qalqalah

Hamzatul-wasl

الجزء الثلاثون سورة العصر

سورة العصر

بِسْمِ اللَّهِ الرَّحْمَٰنِ الرَّحِيمِ

وَالْعَصْرِ ۝ إِنَّ الْإِنسَانَ لَفِي خُسْرٍ ۝ إِلَّا الَّذِينَ آمَنُوا وَعَمِلُوا الصَّالِحَاتِ وَتَوَاصَوْا بِالْحَقِّ وَتَوَاصَوْا بِالصَّبْرِ ۝

سورة الهمزة

بِسْمِ اللَّهِ الرَّحْمَٰنِ الرَّحِيمِ

وَيْلٌ لِّكُلِّ هُمَزَةٍ لُّمَزَةٍ ۝ الَّذِي جَمَعَ مَالًا وَعَدَّدَهُ ۝ يَحْسَبُ أَنَّ مَالَهُ أَخْلَدَهُ ۝ كَلَّا ۖ لَيُنبَذَنَّ فِي الْحُطَمَةِ ۝ وَمَا أَدْرَاكَ مَا الْحُطَمَةُ ۝ نَارُ اللَّهِ الْمُوقَدَةُ ۝ الَّتِي تَطَّلِعُ عَلَى الْأَفْئِدَةِ ۝ إِنَّهَا عَلَيْهِم مُّؤْصَدَةٌ ۝ فِي عَمَدٍ مُّمَدَّدَةٍ ۝

سورة الفيل

بِسْمِ اللَّهِ الرَّحْمَٰنِ الرَّحِيمِ

أَلَمْ تَرَ كَيْفَ فَعَلَ رَبُّكَ بِأَصْحَابِ الْفِيلِ ۝ أَلَمْ يَجْعَلْ كَيْدَهُمْ فِي تَضْلِيلٍ ۝ وَأَرْسَلَ عَلَيْهِمْ طَيْرًا أَبَابِيلَ ۝ تَرْمِيهِم بِحِجَارَةٍ مِّن سِجِّيلٍ ۝ فَجَعَلَهُمْ كَعَصْفٍ مَّأْكُولٍ ۝

سُورَةُ قُرَيْشٍ

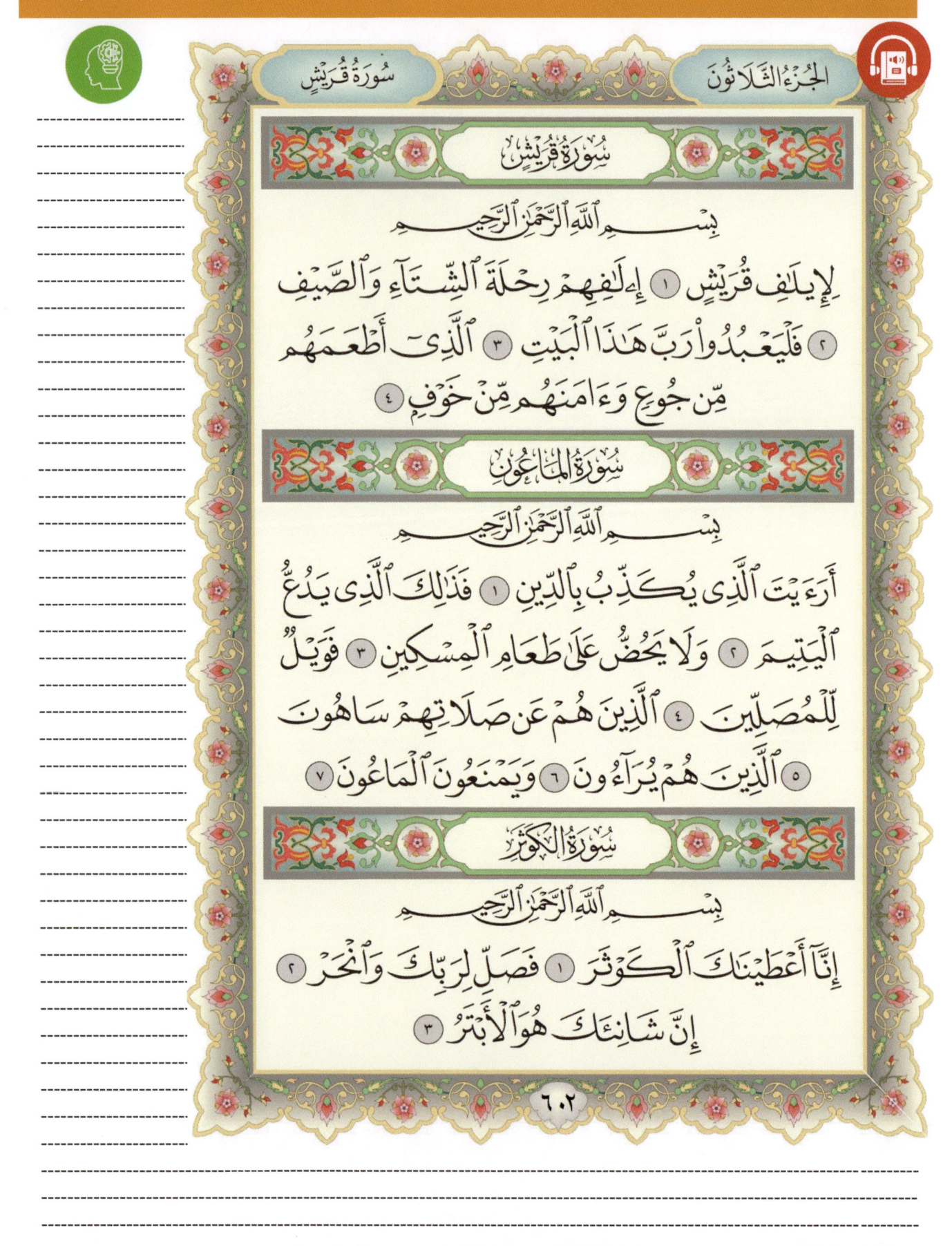

بِسْمِ اللَّهِ الرَّحْمَٰنِ الرَّحِيمِ

لِإِيلَافِ قُرَيْشٍ ۝١ إِيلَافِهِمْ رِحْلَةَ الشِّتَاءِ وَالصَّيْفِ ۝٢ فَلْيَعْبُدُوا رَبَّ هَٰذَا الْبَيْتِ ۝٣ الَّذِي أَطْعَمَهُم مِّن جُوعٍ وَآمَنَهُم مِّنْ خَوْفٍ ۝٤

سُورَةُ الْمَاعُونِ

بِسْمِ اللَّهِ الرَّحْمَٰنِ الرَّحِيمِ

أَرَأَيْتَ الَّذِي يُكَذِّبُ بِالدِّينِ ۝١ فَذَٰلِكَ الَّذِي يَدُعُّ الْيَتِيمَ ۝٢ وَلَا يَحُضُّ عَلَىٰ طَعَامِ الْمِسْكِينِ ۝٣ فَوَيْلٌ لِّلْمُصَلِّينَ ۝٤ الَّذِينَ هُمْ عَن صَلَاتِهِمْ سَاهُونَ ۝٥ الَّذِينَ هُمْ يُرَاءُونَ ۝٦ وَيَمْنَعُونَ الْمَاعُونَ ۝٧

سُورَةُ الْكَوْثَرِ

بِسْمِ اللَّهِ الرَّحْمَٰنِ الرَّحِيمِ

إِنَّا أَعْطَيْنَاكَ الْكَوْثَرَ ۝١ فَصَلِّ لِرَبِّكَ وَانْحَرْ ۝٢ إِنَّ شَانِئَكَ هُوَ الْأَبْتَرُ ۝٣

My Juz' 'Amma Journey

Surah Quraysh shows Allah's favours upon the tribe of Quraysh, and what they were meant to do as a result of that.

	1, 2. For the familiarity of Quraysh with their winter journey to the south and summer journey to the north, We made them safe in their caravans, travelling without any fear.
	3. So let them worship the Lord of the Ka'bah in Makkah.
	4. He is the One Who fed them after hunger, and made them safe after fear.

Surah al-Ma'un mentions the qualities of the rejectors of the afterlife.

	1. Have you seen him who denies the questioning of the Last Day?
	2. That is he who tells off the orphan.
	3. And does not encourage the feeding of the poor.
	4, 5. So woe unto the hypocrites who perform prayers improperly by delaying them from their fixed times.
	6. And who do good deeds only to show off.
	7. And refuse to give the small kindnesses (e.g. salt, sugar, water, etc.).

Surah al-Kawthar highlights Allah's favour upon His Prophet ﷺ and promises his haters of destruction.

	1. We have granted you O Messenger ﷺ a river in Paradise called Al-Kauthar.
	2. So, turn to your Lord in prayer, and sacrifice to Him only.
	3. Indeed, your haters are cut off from every goodness and will be forgotten.

الجزء الثلاثون — سورة قريش

سُورَةُ قُرَيْشٍ

بِسْمِ اللَّهِ الرَّحْمَٰنِ الرَّحِيمِ

لِإِيلَافِ قُرَيْشٍ ۝١ إِيلَافِهِمْ رِحْلَةَ الشِّتَاءِ وَالصَّيْفِ ۝٢ فَلْيَعْبُدُوا رَبَّ هَٰذَا الْبَيْتِ ۝٣ الَّذِي أَطْعَمَهُم مِّن جُوعٍ وَآمَنَهُم مِّنْ خَوْفٍ ۝٤

سُورَةُ الْمَاعُونِ

بِسْمِ اللَّهِ الرَّحْمَٰنِ الرَّحِيمِ

أَرَأَيْتَ الَّذِي يُكَذِّبُ بِالدِّينِ ۝١ فَذَٰلِكَ الَّذِي يَدُعُّ الْيَتِيمَ ۝٢ وَلَا يَحُضُّ عَلَىٰ طَعَامِ الْمِسْكِينِ ۝٣ فَوَيْلٌ لِّلْمُصَلِّينَ ۝٤ الَّذِينَ هُمْ عَن صَلَاتِهِمْ سَاهُونَ ۝٥ الَّذِينَ هُمْ يُرَاءُونَ ۝٦ وَيَمْنَعُونَ الْمَاعُونَ ۝٧

سُورَةُ الْكَوْثَرِ

بِسْمِ اللَّهِ الرَّحْمَٰنِ الرَّحِيمِ

إِنَّا أَعْطَيْنَاكَ الْكَوْثَرَ ۝١ فَصَلِّ لِرَبِّكَ وَانْحَرْ ۝٢ إِنَّ شَانِئَكَ هُوَ الْأَبْتَرُ ۝٣

٦٠٢

My Juz' 'Amma Journey

Write down as many examples as you can from the page:

Identify Makharij of 6 letters	Ghunnah	Madd	Elevated sounds

Noon Saakin & Tanween

Idgham: ------------------

Ikhfaa': ------------------

Iqlab: ------------------

Meem Saakin

Idgham: ------------------

Ikhfaa': ------------------

Qalqalah

Hamzatul-wasl

My Juz' 'Amma Journey

Surah al-Kafirun establishes devotion in worship to Allah alone, together with declaring complete difference between Islam and other religions.

1. Say: "O disbelievers!

2, 3. I don't worship what you worship, and you don't worship Whom I worship.

4, 5. And I don't follow your way of worship, and you don't follow my way of worship.

6. You have your own religion, and I have my own religion."

Surah an-Nasr states that Allah's help is the absolute reason of victory. It also indicates the closeness of the death of the Prophet ﷺ.

1. When Allah's Help comes to you O Messenger and you conquer Makkah.

2. And you see people are entering Allah's religion in crowds,

3. Then, glorify the Praises of your Lord and ask for His Forgiveness. For, indeed, He is the One Who accepts the repentance and forgives.

Surah al-Masad promises the enemies of Islam of disgrace and punishment in this world and the afterlife. Abu Lahab and his wife are included here because of how bad of enemies they were to the Prophet ﷺ.

1. Abu Lahab's two hands will perish, and he himself will perish.

2. His wealth and children will not benefit him.

3. He will be burnt in a Fire of blazing flames!

4. And his wife, who carried thorny wood and put them on the Prophet's way ﷺ, will perish too.

5. She will be humiliated with a twisted rope of palm fibre around her neck.

89

سُورَةُ الْكَافِرُونَ

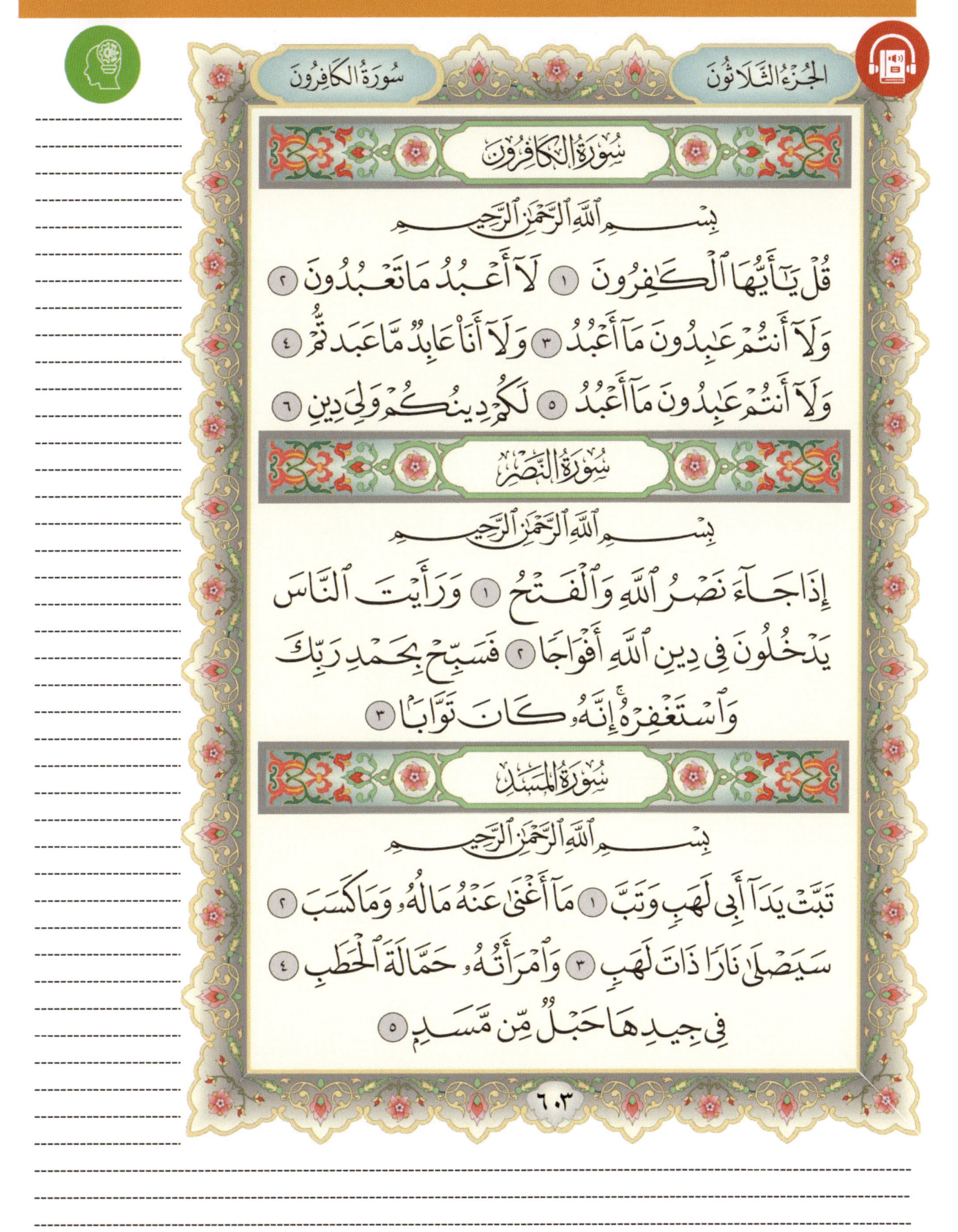

بِسْمِ اللَّهِ الرَّحْمَٰنِ الرَّحِيمِ

قُلْ يَٰٓأَيُّهَا ٱلْكَٰفِرُونَ ۝١ لَآ أَعْبُدُ مَا تَعْبُدُونَ ۝٢ وَلَآ أَنتُمْ عَٰبِدُونَ مَآ أَعْبُدُ ۝٣ وَلَآ أَنَا۠ عَابِدٌ مَّا عَبَدتُّمْ ۝٤ وَلَآ أَنتُمْ عَٰبِدُونَ مَآ أَعْبُدُ ۝٥ لَكُمْ دِينُكُمْ وَلِيَ دِينِ ۝٦

سُورَةُ النَّصْرِ

بِسْمِ اللَّهِ الرَّحْمَٰنِ الرَّحِيمِ

إِذَا جَآءَ نَصْرُ ٱللَّهِ وَٱلْفَتْحُ ۝١ وَرَأَيْتَ ٱلنَّاسَ يَدْخُلُونَ فِى دِينِ ٱللَّهِ أَفْوَاجًا ۝٢ فَسَبِّحْ بِحَمْدِ رَبِّكَ وَٱسْتَغْفِرْهُ ۚ إِنَّهُۥ كَانَ تَوَّابًۢا ۝٣

سُورَةُ الْمَسَدِ

بِسْمِ اللَّهِ الرَّحْمَٰنِ الرَّحِيمِ

تَبَّتْ يَدَآ أَبِى لَهَبٍ وَتَبَّ ۝١ مَآ أَغْنَىٰ عَنْهُ مَالُهُۥ وَمَا كَسَبَ ۝٢ سَيَصْلَىٰ نَارًا ذَاتَ لَهَبٍ ۝٣ وَٱمْرَأَتُهُۥ حَمَّالَةَ ٱلْحَطَبِ ۝٤ فِى جِيدِهَا حَبْلٌ مِّن مَّسَدٍۭ ۝٥

٦٠٣

My Juz' 'Amma Journey

Write down as many examples as you can from the page:

Identify Makharij of 6 letters	Ghunnah	Madd	Elevated sounds

Noon Saakin & Tanween
Idgham: ----------------------

Ikhfaa': ----------------------

Iqlab: ----------------------

Meem Saakin
Idgham: ----------------------

Ikhfaa': ----------------------

Qalqalah

Hamzatul-wasl

سُورَةُ الْكَافِرُونَ

بِسْمِ اللَّهِ الرَّحْمَٰنِ الرَّحِيمِ

قُلْ يَا أَيُّهَا الْكَافِرُونَ ۝ لَا أَعْبُدُ مَا تَعْبُدُونَ ۝ وَلَا أَنْتُمْ عَابِدُونَ مَا أَعْبُدُ ۝ وَلَا أَنَا عَابِدٌ مَا عَبَدْتُمْ ۝ وَلَا أَنْتُمْ عَابِدُونَ مَا أَعْبُدُ ۝ لَكُمْ دِينُكُمْ وَلِيَ دِينِ ۝

سُورَةُ النَّصْرِ

بِسْمِ اللَّهِ الرَّحْمَٰنِ الرَّحِيمِ

إِذَا جَاءَ نَصْرُ اللَّهِ وَالْفَتْحُ ۝ وَرَأَيْتَ النَّاسَ يَدْخُلُونَ فِي دِينِ اللَّهِ أَفْوَاجًا ۝ فَسَبِّحْ بِحَمْدِ رَبِّكَ وَاسْتَغْفِرْهُ ۚ إِنَّهُ كَانَ تَوَّابًا ۝

سُورَةُ الْمَسَدِ

بِسْمِ اللَّهِ الرَّحْمَٰنِ الرَّحِيمِ

تَبَّتْ يَدَا أَبِي لَهَبٍ وَتَبَّ ۝ مَا أَغْنَىٰ عَنْهُ مَالُهُ وَمَا كَسَبَ ۝ سَيَصْلَىٰ نَارًا ذَاتَ لَهَبٍ ۝ وَامْرَأَتُهُ حَمَّالَةَ الْحَطَبِ ۝ فِي جِيدِهَا حَبْلٌ مِنْ مَسَدٍ ۝

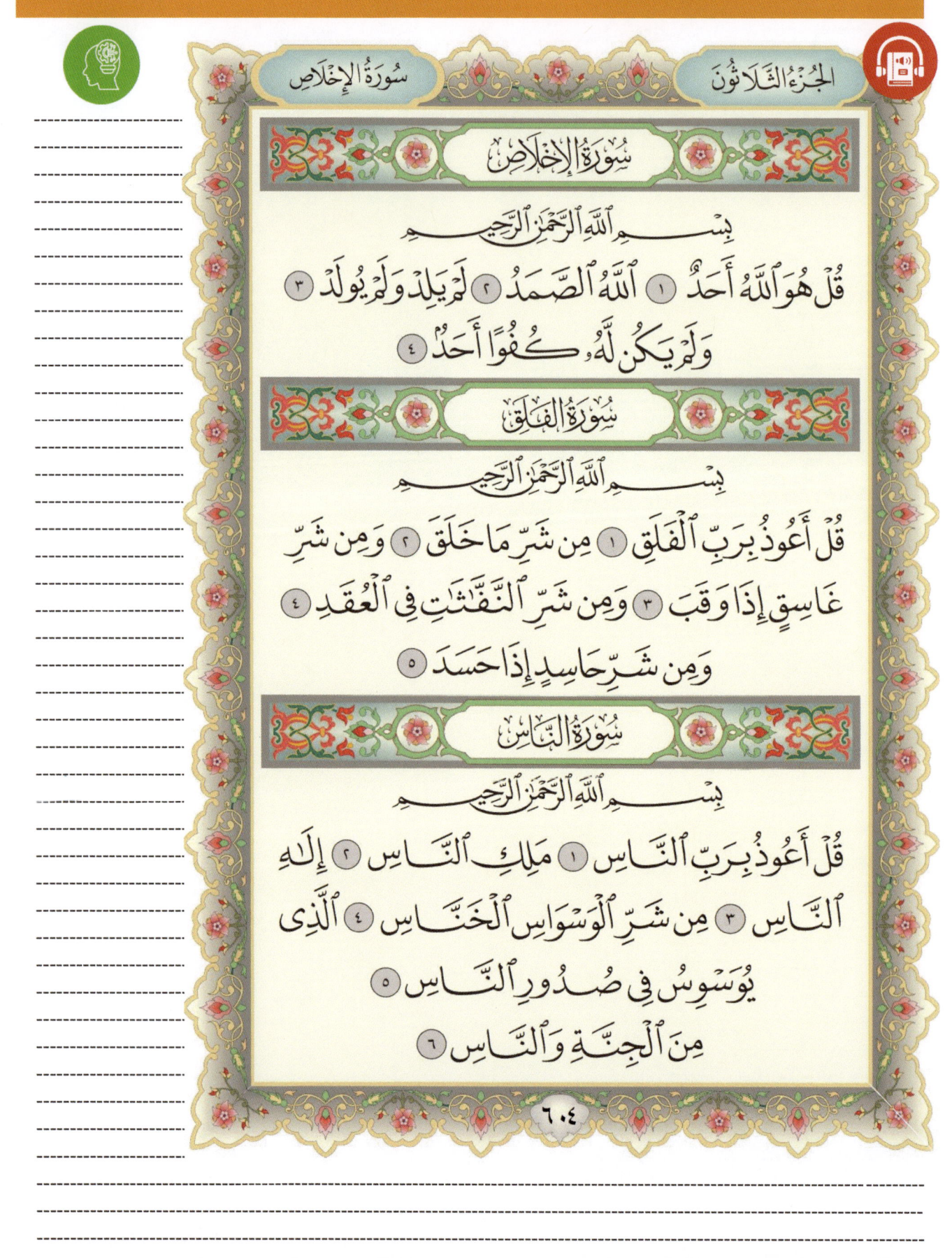

سُورَةُ الْإِخْلَاصِ

بِسْمِ اللَّهِ الرَّحْمَٰنِ الرَّحِيمِ

قُلْ هُوَ اللَّهُ أَحَدٌ ۝١ اللَّهُ الصَّمَدُ ۝٢ لَمْ يَلِدْ وَلَمْ يُولَدْ ۝٣ وَلَمْ يَكُنْ لَهُ كُفُوًا أَحَدٌ ۝٤

سُورَةُ الْفَلَقِ

بِسْمِ اللَّهِ الرَّحْمَٰنِ الرَّحِيمِ

قُلْ أَعُوذُ بِرَبِّ الْفَلَقِ ۝١ مِنْ شَرِّ مَا خَلَقَ ۝٢ وَمِنْ شَرِّ غَاسِقٍ إِذَا وَقَبَ ۝٣ وَمِنْ شَرِّ النَّفَّاثَاتِ فِي الْعُقَدِ ۝٤ وَمِنْ شَرِّ حَاسِدٍ إِذَا حَسَدَ ۝٥

سُورَةُ النَّاسِ

بِسْمِ اللَّهِ الرَّحْمَٰنِ الرَّحِيمِ

قُلْ أَعُوذُ بِرَبِّ النَّاسِ ۝١ مَلِكِ النَّاسِ ۝٢ إِلَٰهِ النَّاسِ ۝٣ مِنْ شَرِّ الْوَسْوَاسِ الْخَنَّاسِ ۝٤ الَّذِي يُوَسْوِسُ فِي صُدُورِ النَّاسِ ۝٥ مِنَ الْجِنَّةِ وَالنَّاسِ ۝٦

My Juz' 'Amma Journey

Surah al-Ikhlas teaches us about Allah's Oneness and perfection.

1. Say: "He is Allah, the One.

2. Allah is the Self-Sufficient Master, Whom all creatures need.

3, 4. He has no children nor parents; and none is like Him."

Surah al-Falaq teaches us to seek Allah's protection from the different apparent evils.

1. Say: "I seek protection of Allah, the Lord of the morning.

2. From any evil that's created.

3. And from the evil that takes place in darkness of night.

4. And from the evil of the witchcrafts when they blow in the knots,

5. And from the evil of the jealous when he gets jealous."

Surah an-Nas teaches us to seek Allah's protection from the evils of Satan and his whispers, and from all hidden evils.

1. Say: "I seek protection of Allah, the Lord of mankind, the King of mankind, the God of mankind.

4. From the evil of the Satan who whispers evil in our hearts, and who runs away when we remember Allah.

5, 6. The Satan who whispers in our hearts can be from jinn or humans."

My Juz' 'Amma Journey

الجزءُ الثلاثونَ سورةُ الإخلاصِ

سورةُ الإخلاصِ

بِسْمِ اللَّهِ الرَّحْمَٰنِ الرَّحِيمِ

قُلْ هُوَ اللَّهُ أَحَدٌ ۝ اللَّهُ الصَّمَدُ ۝ لَمْ يَلِدْ وَلَمْ يُولَدْ ۝ وَلَمْ يَكُن لَّهُ كُفُوًا أَحَدٌ ۝

سورةُ الفلقِ

بِسْمِ اللَّهِ الرَّحْمَٰنِ الرَّحِيمِ

قُلْ أَعُوذُ بِرَبِّ الْفَلَقِ ۝ مِن شَرِّ مَا خَلَقَ ۝ وَمِن شَرِّ غَاسِقٍ إِذَا وَقَبَ ۝ وَمِن شَرِّ النَّفَّاثَاتِ فِي الْعُقَدِ ۝ وَمِن شَرِّ حَاسِدٍ إِذَا حَسَدَ ۝

سورةُ الناسِ

بِسْمِ اللَّهِ الرَّحْمَٰنِ الرَّحِيمِ

قُلْ أَعُوذُ بِرَبِّ النَّاسِ ۝ مَلِكِ النَّاسِ ۝ إِلَٰهِ النَّاسِ ۝ مِن شَرِّ الْوَسْوَاسِ الْخَنَّاسِ ۝ الَّذِي يُوَسْوِسُ فِي صُدُورِ النَّاسِ ۝ مِنَ الْجِنَّةِ وَالنَّاسِ ۝

٦٠٤

My Juz' 'Amma Journey

Write down as many examples as you can from the page:

Identify Makharij of 6 letters	Ghunnah	Madd	Elevated sounds
_____	_____	_____	_____
_____	_____	_____	_____
_____	_____	_____	_____
_____	_____	_____	_____
_____	_____	_____	_____

Noon Saakin & Tanween	Meem Saakin	Qalqalah	Hamzatul-wasl
Idgham: _____	Idgham: _____	_____	_____
Ikhfaa': _____	Ikhfaa': _____	_____	_____
Iqlab: _____		_____	_____

Brief Tajweed

NOTES

Makharij of the letters

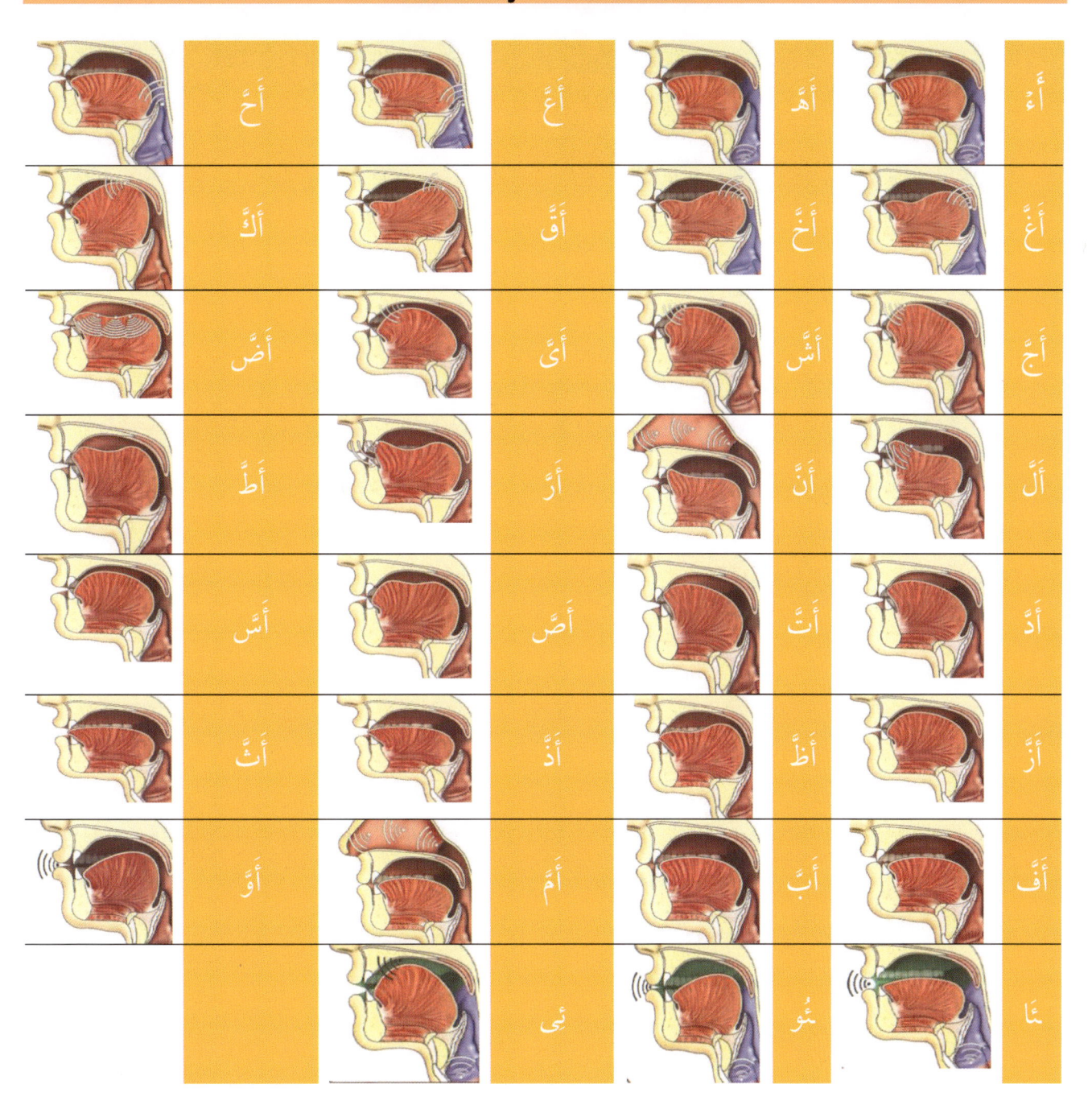

أَحّ		أَعّ		أَهّ		أَءّ	
أَكّ		أَقّ		أَخّ		أَغّ	
أَضّ		أَيّ		أَشّ		أَجّ	
أَطّ		أَرّ		أَنّ		أَلّ	
أَسّ		أَصّ		أَتّ		أَدّ	
أَثّ		أَذّ		أَظّ		أَزّ	
أَوّ		أَمّ		أَبّ		أَفّ	
		ئِيْ		ئُوْ		ئَا	

Ghunnah

Ghunnah is a nasal sound. The two letters that come with ghunnah are (ن and م). When these two letters come with shaddah, ghunnah becomes stronger and longer.

Madd

Simply, when you see a wave sign (~) on top of a madd letter (ا و ى), stretch it for longer time. It can be followed by
- Hamzah, then stretch it for 4 counts.
- Sukoon or shaddah, then stretch it for 6 counts.

Elevated sounds

In Arabic, we have 7 letters which are always elevated (dark). They are:
ق and غ, خ, ظ, ط, ض, ص
We have 3 other letters that are sometimes dark and some other time light:
- ر is generally elevated when it is with fat-hah or dammah. And it is light if it is with kasrah. If it has sukoon, then look at the vowel before it.
- ل of Allah is elevated when there is fat-hah or dammah before it. And it is light if there is kasrah before it.
- ا (the madd letter) follows what is before it.

The rest of the letters are always light.

Noon Saakin & Tanween

Both noon saakin and tanween have the same rules. The way how you read them depends on the letter that comes after them:
- Idgham with ghunnah: Merge them to the letter after, if it is ن, م, و and ى; and apply ghunnah.
- Idgham without ghunnah: Merge them to the letter after, if it is ر ل without making ghunnah.
- Iqlab: Read them as meem with ghunnah if they get ب after them.
- Ikhfaa: Hide the sound of noon saakin and tanween with applying ghunnah if they are followed by one of these 15 letters: ت, ث, ج, د, ذ, ز, س, ش, ص, ض, ط, ظ, ف, ق and ك.
- Idh-har: Other than this, read them clearly. Namely with: ء, ه, ع, ح, غ and خ.

Meem Saakin

We read meem saakin in one of these ways:

- ❖ Idgham: Merge it to the letter after if it is م.
- ❖ Ikhfaa: Hide the sound of م if it has ب after it.
- ❖ Idh-har: Other than this, read it clearly.

Qalqalah

Qalqalah is an echo that happens to five letters (ق ط ب ج د) when they are with sukoon:

- ❖ If the letter comes in the middle of your pronunciation, qalqalah will be weak.
- ❖ If the letter comes in the end of your pronunciation, qalqalah will be strong.

Hamzatul-wasl

In joining, we don't read hamzatul-was. But in starting, read it:

- ❖ ءَ if the definite laam of (al) comes after it.
- ❖ ءُ if letter number 3 has dammah.
- ❖ ءِ if letter number 3 has fat-hah or kasrah.

Printed in Great Britain
by Amazon